D1453572

GAME PLANS
FOR CHILDREN

RAISING A BRIGHTER CHILD
IN 10 MINUTES A DAY

198

Jeanne K. Hanson

G. P. Putnam's Sons
New York

This book is dedicated to my husband,
Burton Randall Hanson, and my children,
Jennifer Hanson and Erik Hanson

Library of Congress Cataloging in Publication Data

Hanson, Jeanne K.
Gameplans for children.

1. Play. 2. Education games. 3. Domestic
education. I. Title.
HQ782.H35 1981   649'.5   81-8489
ISBN 0-399-12670-8   AACR2

Printed in the United States of America

Contents

Chapter Three: Basic Concepts 57

Chapter Four: Basic Knowledge 69

Chapter Nine: Music 130

Chapter Ten: Science Tricks 138

Introduction: What Is the Plan?

This book is especially designed for parents who sometimes have the nagging feeling that they should be spending more time with their children, helping them to learn more. It presents a plan that can fit into anybody's busy schedule because it requires only ten minutes a day: five minutes for Mini-School and five minutes for Family Creativity Time. By using it regularly, you can quite dramatically—and pleasantly—improve your child's school preparation skills and creativity. You *can* teach your child a lot in that amount of time, whether or not you have ever thought of yourself as a teacher.

Even if your child is still a baby—less than one year old—you can begin with the simplest Mini-School learning games, like those that show the difference between the concepts "under the baby" and "over the baby" and those that point out common objects around the house. Many of the games designed for older children to master can also be used as demonstrations to encourage a baby's verbal and conceptual development.

Toddlers—children one and two years old—can learn from a great many of the games here. Some teach basic concepts of texture; others help your child discover which objects "sink, dissolve or float" in water; and still others build left-to-right habits for later reading. Again, verbal and conceptual development are aided.

Preschoolers—three, four and five years old—will be challenged to review some of the earlier games. Then they can further their learning capacities with all the games that build oral, written and visual literacy as well as the skills necessary for advanced learning. They will advance far in their verbal and conceptual skills.

Under the plan, a parent chooses, for each Mini-School day, one of the more than 400 learning games described in the fifteen Mini-School chapters of the book. They add up to a complete, basic, school-style curriculum program of verbal and conceptual skills for your child's preschool years, especially since many of the games are to be repeated periodically for review.

The second part of the plan, Family Creativity Time, is equally important because it encourages your child to exercise his or her imagination. The sessions encourage brainstorming on such subjects as having only one hand, naming a new flavor of strawberry ice cream or telling a story about a very bad child. Choose, for each session, one or two examples like these from the nearly 300 suggested activities located in the eleven family creativity chapters. (Family members will soon be suggesting variants as well as totally new sessions.) The whole family "goes creative" together, having a lot of laughs and promoting family togetherness in the process.

All this—both Mini-School and Family Creativity Time—takes only ten minutes a day of your undivided attention—five minutes for the child's Mini-School and five minutes for the whole family's creativity time. If you have two children, it will be fifteen minutes. With this investment of quality time, your child or children will gradually learn a great deal in an enjoyable way.

WHY DO IT?

My husband and I both work. Our days are crammed with commuting, jobs, home maintenance and caring for our two children. We don't have very much time or energy for formal teaching, even though we believe it to be important. But we don't want the television set, the baby sitter or even our children's preschool teachers to be their *only* teachers. So I've managed to find five minutes a day, per child, to be their "teacher"—to hold Mini-School. My husband and I also spend another five minutes a day with our children in Family Creativity Time. We do both of these five days a week. (We could do it every day, but nobody's perfect.) Nevertheless, we are consistent—this is part of our weekday routine. Naturally, we also spend more time with our children—as camp counselors, referees, overgrown playmates, negotiators, cooks, educational consultants, nurses and so on.

Ten minutes a day may not sound like much time. It certainly does not create an overemphasis on school skills and creativity at the expense of play or other activities. But just think—ten minutes is a long time if you spend it staring out the window, kissing or running at top speed. It is surely a long time from the perspective of a young child. And it can be plenty of time, too, if you regularly spend five minutes of it in a planned learning-games session with your child and another five minutes in a creativity session. Many days the time will fly by. But even on days when it doesn't seem to, it is still manageable.

On most days my two children clamor, "Is it my day to have first 'mini'?" I've even heard, "Let's clean up fast so we can have Family Creativity Time."

Besides teaching your child skills and confidence, this plan benefits parents. Although I have never felt especially guilty about working, I have been particularly guilt-free since we started holding Mini-School and Family Creativity Time. My children are learning a lot, and I feel good about it. On hectic days, the learning games and creativity time can even seem like the only calm moments. Although Mini-School is my responsibility, my husband proudly participates in Family Creativity Time (which was his idea to begin with).

WHAT THIS BOOK WILL NOT DO

The plan covers school preparation skills and creativity quite well, but it is absolutely *not* a blueprint for spending a total of only ten minutes a day with your child. It is not a method for fast toilet-training, nor is it a shortcut to artistic expression, a provision for physical exercise or a quick way of teaching moral values. Neither does it encompass reading to your child, cuddling, taking educational trips, talking about feelings or stopping to smell the daisies. All of these are very important and need to be done in addition to the plan presented here.

Activities like the ones above cannot be done in a few scheduled minutes during the day. Arts and crafts and physical exercise, for example, usually take longer and probably should not be directed by the parent in a "school" atmosphere. Reading to your child nearly every day and going on trips frequently take a long time. And stressing values and talking about feelings are best done unscheduled—close to the time when the child encounters a conflict over such things as lying, or feels anger or pride.

PART I OF THE PLAN, MINI-SCHOOL LEARNING GAMES

Mini-School, presented in detail in Part I, is a series of hundreds of learning games in fifteen key areas—basic things, basic actions, basic concepts, basic knowledge, pre-reading, pre-writing, daily life, visual information, music, science tricks, the basic community, numbers, writing, fun facts and how to find them and reading. It can be held with a child of any age, as long as the learning game selection and atmosphere are appropriate. And the parent does not have to be a formally trained teacher or an expert in any area to do it.

Almost all of the learning games can be done easily at home. At least ninety-five percent of them require no more elaborate equipment than a piece of paper, a pencil, occasionally a child's book—and a child and a parent. A few can be done outside, fewer still while commuting.

The parent chooses, for each Mini-School session, five minutes worth of activities. This will usually consist of one of the learning games from Part I. If your child finishes it early, review it or start another game. If it seems too advanced, choose a simpler game. To gauge better which games will be most appropriate for your child's age, check the "What, Why and Who" section of each Mini-School chapter before delving into that chapter's games. It sketches which games are best for babies, toddlers and preschoolers. When in doubt, start with what you think will be too simple rather than too difficult.

Each game should be used more than once, too. As your child develops, you will be reviewing many of them—especially those that seem a bit too complex the first time, those easily forgotten and even, occasionally, special favorites. "Practice makes perfect" is an old precept now back in favor with many educational psychologists.

Throughout the Mini-School section of the book, the skill areas and game groups within each chapter grow generally more advanced. Therefore, both the beginning Mini-School chapters (especially the first three—Basic

Things, Basic Actions and Basic Concepts) and the beginning games of many of the other early chapters are appropriate for babies. The entire first four chapters are appropriate for toddlers, too, as well as the early game groups within the middle Mini-School skill areas. Preschool children will need to review—quickly, with you— games within the first four chapters that they may not have mastered or may have forgotten. Then they can proceed through the rest of the Mini-School chapters in any order.

Remember that these indications of "baby" (less than a year old), "toddler" (one and two) and "preschooler" (three, four and five) are only rough ones. This is deliberate. Children vary so much. Your three-year-old may need more practice on basic concepts, but may be writing the alphabet letters beautifully and may be speaking in complex sentences. He or she may also be a bit advanced in motor skills or perhaps a bit behind in social skills. (These latter are not a focus of this book— most of them cannot be taught well in short scheduled periods of time.) All this might be the opposite of what your neighbor's child is doing. Don't worry about it. Draw from a variety of Mini-School areas, and jump back and forth for fun as well.

There will be some days when your child prefers a slightly simpler activity or a more exotic one than you have chosen, or may even say, "I want to do writing today." The "teacher" should be flexible.

The atmosphere of Mini-School is as important as the learning games you choose. It should be warm, friendly, encouraging and a little bit challenging. Extra hugs are surely in order when your child suddenly discovers that words are made up of those old familiar letter sounds put together or when he or she counts to forty. A child who masters something a little bit difficult or even concentrates well deserves to feel special pride.

But pressuring or scolding your child is a bad idea. You don't want to make him or her think that school is an ordeal. If you have chosen a game that seems too difficult, just announce, "Oh, that one's supposed to be for bigger kids," and switch to a different game immediately. When in doubt, begin with one you are pretty sure your child can do. And if a child is having an exceptionally bad day in general and cannot even be enticed by a special learning game, you may have to skip "mini" completely. (This should happen only very rarely.)

The "teacher" should give his or her child undivided attention. Set up a table and two chairs in the same room every day—and shut the door. If you're especially efficient, you can even start school at the same time every day so that your child expects it. It's worthwhile, too, to make sure that your other child's or children's needs are taken care of ahead of time so that you won't be interrupted. (Who wants to see wet jeans minutes later on the child who "knew" he shouldn't interrupt his big sister's "mini"?)

Mini-School can also serve as a good preparation for the rules of later school, when, for better or worse, children often have to "do what the teacher says." Since you are the teacher now, you can enforce this part of the atmosphere with some latitude. If your child is feeling especially independent, tactfully begin with a very favorite game. (When our second child was two, he'd always rush in, no matter what, for "sink, dissolve or float" in Chapter Four: Basic Knowledge, partly because he knew he'd get to taste the results if he answered the problem correctly. A sunken almond, dissolved honey and a floating marshmallow were one "very bad day" edible variant—all in the interests of education, of course.) This mild firmness is not only realistic, but is well balanced by the more freewheeling atmosphere of Family Creativity Time.

PART II OF THE PLAN, FAMILY CREATIVITY TIME

Family Creativity Time, presented in Part II, is a series of open-ended, creative sessions in the following eleven areas—what if, name it, I wish, story recipes, body language, say a poem, weird ones, make up a song, produce a show, goofy words and make a family book. They are designed to be played by the whole family together.

Family Creativity Time can be held anywhere at any time. Most sessions require no equipment and can be done at the dinner table or while driving the car. Only Chapter Five: Body Language and Chapter Nine: Produce a Show require moving around; and only Chapters Eight, Nine and Eleven require or suggest any simple supplies.

In spite of some myths, psychologists now say that creativity can be taught. And it is surely worth teaching and practicing for the whole family. Creative thinking is "divergent thinking," or generating a lot of different ideas before you judge any of them as practical, funny or appropriate. So Family Creativity Time provides an especially good balance to Mini-School and to later school, which more often rewards the opposite kind of thinking—"convergent thinking," or zeroing in on one solution to a question or problem. Because the creativity sessions involve the entire family, they also complement the individual emphasis of Mini-School.

The atmosphere should be spontaneous and fun. In a

brainstorming session, people can interrupt each other occasionally. There are no right or wrong answers. Goofiness is fine. Babies are, obviously, observers here, although they can laugh along with the family. But any child who can talk can contribute something. Don't worry if it isn't quite on the subject or sounds a little surrealistic. This kind of mental creativity, unlike the arts and crafts kind, is difficult for two- and even young three-year-olds. So anything goes!

Choose one or two small examples from the areas described in Part II. Or, if you're feeling extra-creative, make up a new one. Older preschoolers will quickly begin to help you do this anyway.

How to Begin

Remember that Mini-School is five minutes of individual learning games for each child every day. This is usually one game.

Skip around. Don't tackle one area for more than a couple of days at a time.

The games tend to get more complex as you proceed through the Mini-School chapters and as you move through the game groups within each Mini-School chapter.

Family Creativity Time is a five-minute, freewheeling session for the whole family. Skip around here, too.

Part I: Mini-School Learning Games

Chapter One: Basic Things

The learning games in this area will introduce your child to the world and to one of its major features—things have names. The kind of names or words explored in the games include—body parts, food, household items, toys, yard items, clothes, car parts and neighborhood features.

The magic of naming has probably been with us since our ancestors grunted in caves or argued around the Tower of Babel. Children participate in this excited "babble" again, in every generation. Even before they can understand a single word, they seem to sense that words go with objects. It is this early sense and interest that you can encourage here.

Babies, who begin by using noises to express themselves, love to hear names for things, too—especially when you, as you hold up something like a ball, look at it, smile and say "ball." In this way even very young babies can play the learning games in this section; it helps them to gradually realize that words go with objects and that the process of naming them is fun for parents and children. This is perhaps their first introduction to the world of concepts and language. Imagine the importance of your child's realization that everything has a name.

Toddlers, even those who can't yet speak but who can understand language, can learn quite a few new words in these games. Older toddlers, those in the "Dat?" and "Wha dat?" stage, will absorb the word games nearly as fast as you can play them. A growing vocabulary helps them to form preliminary group concepts, such as "toy" or "food," as they learn all the examples from the different game groups. With these words and concepts, they can begin to organize their thinking and talking about the world. Reinforced further in Chapter Three: Basic Concepts, these skills will also help your child to build a memory based partly in words. This is a more advanced and more permanent stage of memory than the fleeting images and senses characteristic of a baby's remembrances.

Preschoolers should receive a review here, too. Choose a few games that you think your child might not know. He or she will be building a good base for a large and powerful vocabulary.

Remember that activities within each game group proceed, roughly, from the simpler to the more complicated, as do the game groups themselves. Find five minutes of activities for each Mini-School session.

1 ✳ BODY PARTS, OR WHAT DO YOU HAVE THERE?

Babies can begin to learn the concept of naming here. They will also benefit from the emotional closeness of the games.

Toddlers and preschoolers can learn some extra exotic words and a beginning understanding of what "a body" is. (Although my next statement may sound a bit premature—since drug abuse has yet to hit the tricycle set—

people who have learned early to respect their own bodies *are* much less likely to abuse them by taking drugs later.)

In each case, say the word first, then ask your child to say it (if possible). Then point to the body part and ask your child its name (if possible).

Touch it   Touch your child's mouth, then your own mouth, saying "Judy's mouth," "Mom's mouth." Do the same with these other basic body parts:

nose	ears	hands
fingers	hair	feet
toes	neck	
eyes	tummy	

(To avoid confusion, don't, at this point, teach "head" and other parts that are hard to point to in any one place. And don't use "my" and "your." It is too confusing for a young child to learn that when *you* say *"my* tummy," he or she must change it to *"your* tummy" to mean the same tummy.)

Getting harder   As above, but go on to slightly harder body parts, such as:

elbows	legs	breasts
knees	chest	penis
arms	eyebrows	vagina
heels	eyelashes	

Swing your legs and arms and those of your child to demonstrate that it's the whole limb you're talking about. (And treat the genitals as a normal part of the body, not something to be ashamed of. Introduce nicknames only later and only if you must.)

Fancy body parts   As above, but with:

    ankles
    freckles
    shoulders
    taste buds (with a magnifying glass if you have
        one)
    pupils (point to them in a mirror)
    skin
    bones
    veins (show the blue ones at the wrist)
    corneas (point to them in a mirror)
    wrists
    hairline
    larynx (feel it vibrate through the skin while
        talking)
    ribs (tickle)
    muscles
    thighs

Find it   Have a "Find That Body Part" quiz, asking
your child to find parts from the above games. Just name
a body part and ask your child to touch it. (More games
on the body are found in Chapter Fourteen: Fun Facts
and How to Find Them.)

How they work   Teach your child how some of our
internal organs help us. (Show pictures if you have any
around.)

    The *intestines* help the stomach turn food into
        food energy. Then they take what's left
        and turn it into solid body wastes. (What-
        ever you call it, this is a good time to

teach your child that it is, in fact, material that the body does not need.)

The *bladder* holds the liquid waste until it's ready to come out.

The *lungs* pump air.

The *uterus* is where a baby can grow in a grown-up woman. (Stress that little girls can't grow babies; some have fears about this.)

The *stomach* uses juices called enzymes to dissolve the food we eat, so that it can be turned into food energy. Then we can grow and run. And point out how precious our internal organs are. That's why we don't kick or punch anyone in the stomach area.

The *heart* pumps blood all through our body.

The *brain* thinks, remembers and imagines for us and tells the rest of our body what to do.

2 ✳ FOOD, OR YUM, YUM, WHAT IS IT?

These games teach food names. The best time to play them is right *after* a meal when nobody is hungry.

Tell your child that these are all "food words." Then name the item for the child and ask him or her to repeat it; later, if the child is old enough, point to it and ask the child for its name. (For a different kind of food fun see Chapter Twenty-Two: Weird Ones.)

Cupboard and refrigerator basics   Teach your child the names of common family foods, in and out of their containers. Allow him or her to handle and smell them. Your child will begin to learn the basic concept names for food groups along with individual food names if you teach words like "peachfruit," "applefruit," "bananafruit," "grapesfruit," while explaining that these are all part of a group we call fruit. Once the child has mastered the concept the second word will drop off naturally and easily.

Exotics   Teach the names of the more obscure foods you have on hand, such as vinegar, baking soda, and the like.

Grocery extravaganza   Spend a Mini-School in a grocery store teaching your child the names of some of the foods you don't buy—lamb chops, eggplant, oyster crackers, or whatever.

3 ✳ HOUSEHOLD ITEMS, OR WHAT DO WE HAVE AROUND HERE ANYWAY?

Naming the furniture and other household items will add to your child's "mental furnishings" and help him or her feel more at home in the world of language. Proceed to name the item and have your child repeat it, if possible; later, ask the child to name the item, if possible. (Games on *explaining* household items are found in Chapter Seven: Daily Life and Chapter Eight: Fun Facts and How to Find Them.)

A basic tour   Have your child take you on a tour around the house, pointing to large furniture items for you to identify. Avoid the kitchen for now. Teach by touching and naming:

chair	curtain	door
windows	toilet	TV
dresser or	bookcase	table
bureau	bed	window
sofa or couch		

(Here again you can teach the concept along with the individual item by using "double names" like "dining room table" and "end table.")

Getting harder   As above, but with items like:

mantelpiece	dresser	blanket
pillow	flower pot	closet
bedspread	carpet	mirror
clock	rug	washbasin
vase	picture on the	calendar on
	wall	the wall

The kitchen   As above, but find such items as:

high chair	knife	fork
spoon	cup	glass
plate	bowl	stove
refrigerator	cupboard	can opener
towel rack	spatula	slotted spoon
freezer	dish towel	paper towels
compart-		
ment		

The truly exotic   As above, but with:

    picture hooks   window sill   wallpaper
    molding   archway   paint
    . . . and your full array of cooking supplies.

More   Teach your house's largest features. These tend to be harder to learn than you may imagine because you can't point to any one place:

    entryway   ceilings   halls
    walls   floors   . . . and so
                                       on.

Quiz   Close this session with a "Find That Room" quiz. Your "household detective" has to find, room by room, anything you name.

4 ✳ TOYS, OR WHAT ARE WE PLAYING WITH ANYWAY?

There are lots more names to learn here, beginning with your child's favorite toys. Remember to mention that these are all "toys." And teach the concept or category name along with the specific name ("fire truck" and "garbage truck"; "baby doll" and "Raggedy Ann doll").

Our toys   As your child leads you around the house, you say the name of the toy first, then have your child repeat it, if possible. After that, have him or her identify it, if possible.

5 ✹ YARD THINGS, OR WATCH THAT WORM

For an outdoors Mini-School, point out the following things in the yard and ask your child to repeat their names. Then, later, if your child is old enough, ask him or her to identify them when you point.

What's here By the point-and-say method, teach such items as:

grass	bush	tree
fence	flower	truck
car	sidewalk	sky
clouds	sun	moon
rocks	dirt or mud	bicycle
tricycle	doors	flies
bees	tree branch	worms

Evening version As above, but with:

stars	moon	taillights
streetlights	headlights	moths
a planet, if possible	shadows	

Exotics Same as before, but identify more exotic things such as:

moss	dandelion	crabgrass
twigs	crocus	passserby
ant hill	pedestrian	dragonfly
squirrel	lichen	

6 ✳ CLOTHES, OR WHAT DO WE WEAR?

Many new words are hiding right now in your child's
drawer and even covering parts of his or her body. They
describe your child's clothing. Teach the concept of
clothes first. Then point out the different kinds, asking
your child to repeat each word. Then, if possible, see if
the child can identify them.

You wear   Teach the bigger items first, such as:

pajamas	sleepsack	suspenders
dress	nightie	diaper
pants	underpants	socks
shoes	plastic pants	booties
hat	undershirt	coat
jacket	sweater	shirt

Clothing parts   Same as the above, but move to such
smaller parts as:

zipper	buttonhole	button
snap	hood	cuffs
sleeve	collar	mittens
strap	lace	

Parents' clothes   Next a tour of the parental closet and
dresser:

slip	bra	vest
sport jacket	suit	necklace
bracelet	T-neck shirt	ring
necktie	loafer	sandals
high-heeled shoes	gloves	

Throw it Have a "Throw It" quiz, with your child finding, and throwing up in the air, any clothing item you name. (Then he or she puts each one back where it belongs!)

7 ✳ CAR PARTS, OR HONK HONK

Your child can learn a lot by sitting behind the wheel of a car or even running circles around the entire vehicle—when it is safely parked, of course. Point out the parts; then ask your child to repeat the words, if possible. Afterwards ask him or her to identify the car parts, if this is possible.

It's our car Teach words like:

headlights	taillights	fender
seat	ignition	gear shift
blinker	horn	door handle
flaps	seat lever	windshield wipers
brake pedal	door locks	radio
accelerator pedal	chrome strips	hood

and as many of the parts under the hood as you know. (Since our children are always strapped in while driving, they love to clamber around the interior during Mini-School to "find the part.")

8 ✳ THE NEIGHBORHOOD, OR LET'S GET OUT OF THE HOUSE

Your child can become quite familiar with major features of the neighborhood, especially when you tell him or her the new word, ask to hear it (if possible) and later ask the child to identify the features. (More activities on the neighborhood are found in Chapter Eleven: The Basic Community.)

Major nearby features   Introduce your child to the following (or comparable substitutes):

brick apartment house
skyscraper
gas station
park
drugstore
the Jones's house (for
    several different
    neighbors)

wooden fence
garage
clothing store
sidewalk
grocery store
subway station

Finer details   Also teach:

more stores
hedge
elm trees
park bench
woodpile
alley
freeway or highway

more neighbors'
    names
oak trees
movie theatre
bus stop
garbage cans

Point it out   Have a "Point It Out" quiz, with you pointing and your child naming the various neighborhood features.

Chapter Two: Basic Actions

The learning games in this section teach your child basic actions—what toys do; what's going on outside; what we can do with our bodies; what we look like doing it; and what tools and a few of our household machines can accomplish. Through them, your child can feel that his or her actions produce results and can learn some of the words which describe those actions. This begins to build a sense of power along with a larger vocabulary.

Many of the games are "learn by doing" activities while others require paying attention to the world around you. All involve describing. You first describe the action in a two-word phrase or sentence; your child learns to perform it, and then your child tries to say the two-word description. Once this part of the format is mastered (by about the time your child can perform the last part of game group 3), you begin to elaborate on your child's sentence or phrase. This further extends his or her vocabulary, as described below.

Babies can listen to your descriptions with interest. Older ones can even imitate some of your actions with toys.

Toddlers, especially those near the two-word stage of language ("Ball go," "Mom do," and so on), will use these games to make giant leaps in their word collections and to reinforce and vary their early sentence patterns.

Preschoolers should receive a review of the words here, even in the first three game groups of this section, since they present a quite inclusive vocabulary. Look them over for words you think your child doesn't know and teach all of these in one or two Mini-School sessions. Preschoolers will also benefit from all or most of game groups 4, 5 and 6.

Remember that the later games are more advanced and that the games within a group also proceed, generally, from easy to more difficult. Choose five minutes of activities for each Mini-School session.

1 ✴ Toys Do It, or Make the Keys Clatter

The games here will provide a sense of power and some key vocabulary for your child.

With a baby, you say, for example, "The ball rolls," and demonstrate for your child. With a toddler, you roll the ball and say, "The ball rolls," then ask him or her to do it and, if possible, say the two-word sentence "ball rolls." For an older toddler, say, "Make the ball roll." Then ask him or her to do it and say for you, "ball rolls." (Don't switch your own sentence to "roll the ball" if your child is a toddler; it is harder for him or her to change the order of the words back to "ball rolls.")

Basic Moving   Proceed according to the above instructions, with the following actions:

truck moves	blocks fall
shovel digs	water splashes
drum booms	boat floats

More moving   As above, but with:

keys clatter	water sloshes
dishes clatter	ball bounces
horn toots	rattle rattles

Getting harder   As above, but with:

clock bongs	train clanks
bell rings	paper tears
top spins	car crashes

Review it   Review the phrases by asking your child to clatter, dig, ring, bounce, etc.

2 ✳ OUTSIDE, OR WHAT'S MOVING AROUND OUT HERE

These games teach the words that go with outdoor actions. Included are weather happenings as well as movements your child can perform. They are arranged so that you can include both kinds on a given day. (More of the child's own actions are found in game group 3 of this area.)

The basics I   Proceed according to the format described in the introductory section of game group I and teach:

leaves move	pick leaf
wind blows	ride tricycle
bird flies	throw stick

The basics II   As above, but with:

> rain falls   puddles splash
> thunder booms   lightning crashes

Getting harder I   As above, but with:

> man walks   pick flower
> kids play   scratch tree
> kids shout   find bug

Getting harder II   As above, but with:

> dog runs   dog barks
> woman jogs   kick ball

Different weather   As above, but with:

> snow falls   pat snow
> slush splatters   squeeze snow
> truck honks   make snowball

Three-worders   As above, but with:

> clouds move by   jackhammer drills
> squirrel climbs tree   loud
> lawnmower cuts grass   wind sways trees
> cat walks by

Act it out   Review all these dynamic actions by asking
your child to identify or do them.

3 ✳ HOW WE MOVE INDOORS, OR MOVE IT, KID!

The games here can be done indoors or outdoors and

will further increase your child's vocabulary. Teach your child each action; demonstrate it if necessary, while saying the appropriate word. Then ask your child to perform and describe it, if possible.

What you can do I   Proceed according to the above instructions with these actions:

walk	talk	roll
crawl	laugh	clap hands
jump	swing arms	sing
bend over	rub	shout
kick	nod	

What you can do II   As above, but with:

squat	clap hands	lean to one
crouch	pat	side
chew	scratch	turn a light
stretch	hop	switch on
thump	sniff	and off

More elaborate I   Next, have your child perform the following actions, one by one. As you go along, ask your child to say the basic words while you elaborate on them, as indicated by some samples in parentheses below.

make a fist ("now you look extra strong")
giggle ("ho ho ho, ha ha ha, what's so
    funny?")
pound your fist
turn the pages of a book
bend your elbow

point your toes
flex your arm muscle
twist your wrist
shut the door

More elaborate II   As above, but with:

march around the room ("you look like
    you're in a parade")
listen carefully
gallop
blow your nose
tickle me
whisper in my ear
whap the chair
bow or curtsey
poke the sofa

Truly exotic I   As above, but with:

pinch the upholstery ("now we wouldn't do
    that to our brother, but it's okay here on
    the sofa")
pull the pillow
hang up the telephone
buzz
wobble
dangle
scrub
kneel
slide

The ultimate!   As above, but with:

stamp ("my, you look mad!")

walk on tiptoe
prance
slobber, spit and drool (optional)
cut it in half
stack books
turn the faucet off
whistle (try, anyway)
blink and wink (try)

Do it, big kid   Review the above actions by asking your
child to do them.

4 ✳ REFLECTIONS, OR WHAT DO YOU LOOK LIKE
WHEN YOU'RE DOING ALL THESE THINGS?

To increase your child's awareness of himself or
herself in action, use a full-length or large mirror. Babies
are fascinated with mirrors, and toddlers can really enjoy
them. Make sure to give extra praise here because here
your child is really "on stage."

What is that?   Lead your child up to the mirror. Help
him or her touch, on the glass, his nose, hair, eyes,
mouth, shoulders, stomach and other visible body parts.
Explain to him that this is a "real reflection—it's what
you really look like. But it isn't you. It's like a picture of
you. And it shows what Mom really looks like too,
doesn't it? It's a reflection."
Then have him or her find other body parts in the
reflection.

You're looking good   Choose one of the games in game
group 3 above, and have your child perform the actions in
front of the mirror. Either you or your child should
describe them at the same time.

Sort of   Next show your child his or her "partial reflection" in a large window. Explain that this isn't a mirror, but it's a little like one. Then look at both your reflections in something concave or convex but reflective, such as a chrome flower pot. Explain that this is "weird" and "goofy," that it's a "distorted reflection." It's not a good mirror because we don't really look like that, do we?

5 ✳ TOOLS, OR WHAT DO WE DO WITH THIS THING?

These games will help your child learn more action concepts. He or she will be able to carry out some of them and simply observe others. Let your child do as many of them as you think safely possible, because they will also help to develop eye-hand coordination. This develops gradually. A two-year-old can open a hinged door and spear with a fork. A three-year-old loves to learn to cut with a scissors and paste two things together. But a five-year-old may still have trouble with wrenches and even with cutting an apple.

As you teach the new words, keep pointing out to your child how tools help us to accomplish many tasks and projects. Mention that there are many new tools left to be invented, and add that the child might want to invent a new tool when he or she grows up. (More games on tools and inventions are found in Chapter Fourteen: Fun Facts and How to Find Them.)

The basics   Show your child how to perform each action, ask him or her to perform it while saying the words and then elaborate yourself—with words—on what your child has done. (More detailed instructions are in game group 3 above.) Begin with:

spoon stirs ("you're really a cook now")
knife cuts
door swings on its hinges
fork spears
hammer pounds

A bit tougher   As above, but with:

scissors cut
tape holds two things together
paste holds two things together
glue holds two things together
a pin holds two things together

Quite hard   As above, but with:

a knife spreads
a piece of string ties two things together
a rubber band stretches around something
a rubber band holds two things together

Yipes!   As above, but with:

a needle sews
a screwdriver screws
a wrench twists
a wire whisk beats an egg
an eggbeater beats an egg

Animals and tools   Explain to your child that only a
very few animals use tools. A chimpanzee, for example,
can use a piece of straw to poke into wood to obtain
food. And a few kinds of birds can also use this
implement; they might poke straw into the bark of a tree
to find bugs to eat. There aren't many more examples.

Ask your child *how* a bird could use a straw to poke into tree bark. And *why* would fish have trouble using tools, even if they were smart enough to invent or find them?

6 ✴ MACHINES WORK, OR HANG ON TO THAT MIXER

These games progress from the idea of tools as our helpers to simple machines. Machines are simply tools that use extra power, more "oomph" than what we have in our own hands. (More games on household appliances are found in Chapter Seven: Daily Life.)

Simple machines   Show your child how to operate the following "tools," *with* your help. Teach the words along with the actions (and remind the child to do them only with an adult).

> a blender blends food together
> a mixer beats cake batter
> a vacuum cleaner roars and cleans the rug
> a toaster toasts bread
> . . . and whatever other small, specific appliances you have around

Chapter Three: Basic Concepts

The learning games in this area are designed to help your child develop his or her first real concepts. They begin with the ones "closest to home," particularly those involving the five senses which a child uses even before birth. Specifically, the game groups introduce early concepts of taste, smell, texture, noise, a wide variety of visible sensory opposites, basic shapes, expressions, basic counting, color and the idea of a family.

Your child can use his or her early experiences and those you provide in these games to create the building blocks of thinking. Without concepts, one taste cannot be thought of as being clearly different from another taste, nor can green be classified as a color like yellow or purple. With them, and with the words for them, your child can process, compare and remember experiences many times more clearly.

Even a baby has enough experience to begin to build on here. Your baby's world is not a blooming, buzzing confusion for very long, psychologists now say, although it certainly is a confetti-throw of sensation. Taste is probably our best-developed sense at birth. Studies have shown that even newborns are able to turn away from such strong tastes as vinegar. Hearing and touch are well

57

developed, too, with experience beginning well before birth—even very young babies can turn toward their mothers' voices, psychologists have found. Vision follows. So your baby can appreciate these games and the word play that goes with them.

A toddler is quite experienced at sensation. He or she can, all at once, hear a parent laugh, see a splash of sunshine bright on a high chair tray, taste a soft banana, smell orange juice and feel a wet diaper. A child this age grows fast mentally as a result of classifying these sensations, hearing the words for them and forming concepts.

Even a preschooler can benefit from a review of these games. Some of the words for the opposites and some of the colors will be challenging even for children in this age group.

Activities within each game group, and the game groups themselves, proceed from easier to harder (generally). Choose five minutes of activities for each Mini-School session.

1 ✱ TASTES, OR IS IT YUCKY?

These games can be considered an "appetizer course" before your child's meal, as he or she experiences the differences among the tastes, hears the words connected with them and, if possible, learns to incorporate them into his or her vocabulary.

Sweet and sour   Set out two sweet foods and two sour ones. Have your child taste a tiny bit of each. Say to him or her, for example, "Honey is a sweet food. Candy is a sweet food. Vinegar is a sour food. Mayonnaise is a sour food." Keep the food in or near the original containers so that your child learns to identify them, too.

Then move the foods out of order. Ask your child to taste and tell you which are sweet and which are sour. (Stress that we only taste things in the kitchen with an adult.)

Salty and bland   As above, but use two salty snack foods and two bland foods such as plain bread and bran.

Crunchy and smooth   As above, only try something like nuts and hard candy vs. ice cream and margarine.

A big taste test   Ask your child to take any three foods out of the refrigerator and tell you whether each is sweet or sour, salty or bland, or crunchy or smooth. (Accept combinations and approximations!)

2 ✱ SMELLS, OR DOES YOUR NOSE LIKE IT?

These games require your child to discriminate among smells. Bear in mind that yucky is sometimes in the nose of the sniffer. The classification isn't as important as learning that odors can be very different and that we can associate them with their sources. Remember to point out that we wouldn't eat any of these things unless a grown-up gave them to us.

Because it is not easy for a child to breathe through the nose while keeping the mouth closed, you may need to teach this technique first.

In the kitchen   Let your child smell the following things while you give each name. Then ask whether it smells good or bad.

   all kitchen spices and extracts
   canned, boxed and fresh foods

A sniff tour   As above, but with:

> the insides of various small appliances
> perfumes
> furniture
> basement closets
> books

Outdoors   As above, but with:

grass
dead leaves
tree trunks
bushes

garages
outdoor water
various flowers
asphalt

Snifferooquiz   Blindfold your child and ask him or her to smell various things and identify them.

3 ✸ TEXTURES, OR WHAT DOES IT FEEL LIKE?

These games provide a basic introduction to the words for what one feels with the fingers. (More games on materials found in Chapter Four: Basic Knowledge.)

Rough and smooth   Set out two rough objects, such as a rock and a piece of sandpaper; and two smooth objects, such as a piece of paper and a lid. Tell your child something like, "That is a rough rock. That is rough sandpaper," and so on.

Then switch the objects around and ask the child to touch them and tell you which are rough and which are smooth.

If your child is old enough, ask him or her to find more rough objects and more smooth ones and bring them to you.

Hard and soft   As above, but with a plastic truck and a table, for example, vs. a marshmallow and a pillow.

What's there   When your child is not looking, place one rough, one smooth, one hard and one soft object in a brown paper bag. Leave only enough room at the top for your child to reach in with one hand. Without looking, ask him or her to describe each object as rough or smooth, hard or soft. Then ask the child to tell you the name of each item, once again without looking. Finally, have your child show you the object to see if he or she was correct.

4 ✸ Noises, or Can You Hear One Hand Clapping?

Noises are part of our world and so is silence. The purpose of these games is to teach your child the difference, as well as how to discriminate among sounds.

Loudly and softly   Sing, run water and clap—each loudly, then softly. Tell the child which sound is loud and which is soft.

Then ask him or her to tap a spoon on the table—first loudly, then softly. Then talk both ways. Then laugh both ways.

Silence   The Montessori method makes a good point when it teaches that silence must be learned to be appreciated. A child must learn how to be silent in several steps—no talking, no moving the feet, no moving the arms and so on.

Once this has been mastered, ask your child to listen carefully and to identify noises he or she can now hear—a car? the washing machine? the wind? a sibling? an airplane overhead? etc.

Sound tapping   To help your child learn to identify more sounds, blindfold him or her (if your child finds this frightening, wait until he or she is a few months older). Then ask your child to listen when you tap on an object to figure out, by the sound only, what you are tapping. Tap things like the TV screen, a window, a plastic table, a wooden chair and so on. The child's answers may be substances, like "metal," or objects, like "the chair." Either is fine, but tell the child that it's the substance we really hear—it's a *"wooden* chair," *"metal* lamp pole," *"glass* window," *"plastic* table," etc.

5 ✳ OPPOSITES, OR WHAT DO YOU SAY WHEN YOU DON'T WANT TO SAY YES?

These games teach a wide variety of sensory opposites to help your child interpret and classify familiar experiences and concepts. If your child is inexperienced at this, illustrate what "opposite" means by saying, "No is *the opposite* of yes," "Light switch on is *the opposite* of light switch off," and a couple of other examples close to your child's experience.

Then assemble some of the following objects to illustrate opposites and have your child "act out" the others. (Learning by doing should be used whenever possible, since it is the kind most readily remembered.)

Opposites I   Use objects to demonstrate or act out these opposites with your child.

big vs. little or small   open vs. shut or
                                                    closed

heavy vs. light   loud vs. soft or quiet
dark vs. light   empty vs. full

Opposites II   As above, but with:

fast vs. slow   top vs. bottom
hard vs. soft   in vs. out
push vs. pull   cold vs. warm and
                                        hot

Opposites III   As above, but with:

black vs. white   lock vs. unlock
up vs. down   on vs. off
front vs. back   hungry vs. full

Opposites IV   As above, but with:

under vs. over or above   dirty vs. clean
fat vs. thin or skinny   asleep vs. awake
straight vs. bent or   short vs. tall or long
    crooked

Opposites V   As above, but with:

fix up vs. wreck or mess   in front of vs. behind
    up   rough vs. smooth
forwards vs. backwards   fuzzy vs. smooth
    and sideways   dry vs. wet

Opposites VI   As above, but with:

young vs. old   happy vs. sad
start vs. finish   around vs. through

ugly vs. pretty, beautiful,   beginning vs. end
    or handsome

Opposites VII   As above, but with:

fresh vs. stale or rotten   many vs. few
left vs. right   a lot vs. a little
crazy vs. sane or normal   more vs. less

Opposites quiz   Ask your child to act out or bring
objects to you to illustrate the above opposites.

6 ✳ SHAPES, OR IS THAT REFRIGERATOR A
CIRCLE?

The games here teach your child the shape names of
the objects around us. They will help him or her see the
world in a little different way. At this level, ignore the
issue of two-dimensional as opposed to three-dimensional
objects—use the names for the flat shapes, but add one
key double name—"round circles"—to teach both words.
(More shape games are found in Chapter Seven: Daily
Life.)

Our basics   On a piece of paper, draw a square, a
rectangle, a triangle and a circle. Point out what dis-
tinguishes each ("a square has four straight sides and four
corners," for example) and guide your child's finger
around the edges of each shape. Then you, or the child if
possible, should cut them out so the child can play with
them. Review their names during playtime.

All around us   Ask your child to be your "shape
detective" and lead you around the house, showing you

"round circle-shaped things." Find four together; then look at four squares, four rectangles and four triangles.

Exotics   A commercial "shape toy box" is the easiest tool to use for teaching the more exotic shapes. You might want to give your child, as a birthday or Christmas present, the kind where the child has to match each shape to its hole to drop it inside. With it, teach as many of the shapes as you know!

Or you could draw pentagons, hexagons, octagons, polygons, ovals, stars, rosettes and several kinds of triangles and cut them out with your child.

7 ✹ EXPRESSIONS, OR ARE YOU ANGRY?

These games introduce your child to the early concepts of mood and body language. Your child has seen and responded to people's moods and actions for most of his or her life but may not know how to identify them with words. Also, most children use tone of voice *and* facial expressions *and* movement styles to analyze someone's mood, but may not yet be able to separate these cues and recognize what they signal. (More games on facial expressions are found in Chapter Eight: Visual Information, and sessions on body language are in Chapter Twenty: Body Language.)

For a toddler, act out each expression yourself first, then ask him or her to "be that way," in front of a mirror (if your child is comfortable with mirrors) or just in front of you. Older children can act out all the expressions by themselves.

Faces   Demonstrate the following, giving examples of instances when your child might have looked and felt that way:

happy face	worried face
sad face	excited face
mad face	discouraged face
mean face	proud face

(Then try to remember to point out these faces to your child in books or on television, too.)

Walking styles   As above, but with the following (including the synonym words):

gaily walking
casually walking (strolling or ambling)
proudly walking (strutting)
walking tiredly (trudging)
walking fearfully
walking sneakily (skulking along)
walking hurriedly

8 ❋ BASIC COUNTING, OR HOW MANY EYES DO YOU HAVE?

These games constitute a very basic introduction to the idea of numbers and to the rote repetition of basic numbers. As you introduce your child to counting, begin using numbers in conversation, too, as much as possible. Say, "It's five minutes until dinner," or *"Sesame Street* will start in fifteen minutes," for example, instead of using vague phrases. (For more advanced games on numbers see Chapter Four: Basic Knowledge; Chapter Ten: Science Tricks; Chapter Twelve: Numbers; and Chapter Fourteen: Fun Facts and How to Find Them.)

Numbers are here   For a baby or a toddler, count your own and his or her body parts, in turn. Point to and say, "one eye, two eyes, on Billy"; then "one eye, two eyes, on Mom."

Bigger numbers   Repeat numbers so that your child can learn them, using a child's number book if you have one. Practice from one through ten, then from one through twenty.

9 ✳ COLORS, OR DO YOU HAVE ON PURPLE SOCKS?

The games here are designed to teach your child basic colors. This is much harder to learn than most parents realize. So concentrate at first on only the truest, brightest colors, a few at a time. (A game for the more exotic colors is found in Chapter Eight: Visual Information.)

The primaries   Set out objects in the following colors. Or have the child scribble these colors with crayons on separate pieces of paper. Teach the names. Then ask the child to find something around the house in each of these colors (accept anything close, just remarking, "Yes, that's a dark red"):

> red
> blue
> yellow

More colors   As above, but with:

> green
> orange
> purple

Still more   As above, but with:

> black
> brown
> white

More   As above, but with:

> tan or beige
> pink
> grey

10 ❋ OUR FAMILY, OR HOW MANY MOMS AND DADS WOULD YOU LIKE TO HAVE?

These games introduce your child to the basic idea of a family. But don't expect him or her to really comprehend this concept for several years (a sense of the life span seems to come only with maturity).

Who's who   Ask your child to name the people in your immediate family. Then ask him or her, "Who is *your* Mom? Who is *your* brother?" and so on.

Next proceed to "Who is *my* Mom?" "Who is Billy's sister (you)?" and so on.

Tell your child that a family is a group of people who love each other and often live in the same house.

Who and where   Teach your child the names of more distant relatives and of the cities (or streets, if they live in your town) where they live.

Chapter Four: Basic Knowledge

WHAT, WHY AND WHO

The learning games in this area will help your child learn basic information, from the names of the four seasons to how cookies crumble (literally). They are arranged in the following game groups—basic lists, personal facts, basic materials, basic patterns, counting by rote, special facts and how materials change. (More advanced games along some of these lines are found in Chapter Ten: Science Tricks, Chapter Twelve: Numbers and Chapter Fourteen: Fun Facts and How to Find Them. And the kinds of basic knowledge needed to prepare for reading and writing are found in Chapter Five: Pre-Reading and Chapter Six: Pre-Writing.)

Many of the games here ask your child to memorize and identify. These are rather unglamorous thinking skills, but they are the foundation for more advanced conceptual thinking. After all, no one can analyze ideas or even process facts very well until he or she has a certain amount of basic information with which to work.

Children are almost like sponges—they enjoy memorizing and will absorb this information about as fast as you can provide it. Nevertheless, don't ladle it on to the exclusion of other games, and make sure to help your child review this information in later Mini-School sessions. Just tuck in a few facts under their belts!

Babies can be shown some of these activities, but the games are most suitable for toddlers (especially game groups 3 and 4) and younger preschoolers.

Remember that the later game groups are more advanced and that the games within a group also proceed, roughly, from easier to harder. Choose five minutes of activities for each Mini-School session.

1 ✳ BASIC LISTS, OR MEMORIZE IT, KID!

These games are sheer memory work, the results of which will make your child feel proud. To make the lists easier and more fun to learn, use a song or rhythmic chant, if you can invent one, and come back to these games periodically until you are sure they have been learned.

The four seasons   Teach the names—spring, summer, fall, winter—along with what kind of weather your area has with each. Also point out, for example, that "spring on the calendar" starts on March 20 or 21 each year but that "spring weather" starts gradually and somewhat earlier or later than the calendar date.

Which season is it here now? Also discuss people your child knows who live in areas where the weather and seasons are significantly different from yours.

Days of the week   Teach the seven days of the week. And mention the origin of a couple of the words—such as Sunday, named after the sun, and Monday, named after the moon.

Months of the year I   Have your child learn the twelve

months. Stress that they all come this year, then they all come again next year, and so on every year. That's why you can have a birthday on January 27th, *every* year.

Months of the year II   When your child is old enough to learn more, point out which months have thirty days and which have thirty-one. Then add that February has twenty-eight days for three years in a row and twenty-nine every fourth year, on leap year. Use the little chant, "Thirty days hath September, April, June and November. All the rest have thirty-one, save February which, in time, has twenty-eight or twenty-nine."

You can also explain that our calendar plan comes from the Romans who lived many, many years ago. They figured out how long it takes our earth to go around the sun (365¼ days). That's one year. And then they divided those days into twelve months.

Quiz the basics   Ask your child to reel off the seasons, days of the week and months of the year.

2 ✳ PERSONAL FACTS, OR WHERE DO WE LIVE, ANYWAY?

It is important for your child to know key telephone numbers, his or her address and personal facts. That way, your child can tell them to someone if necessary.

Address and phone   Have the child learn your address, including the zip code, and if applicable, your apartment number and home phone number. Tell him or her that nobody else in the world has our same address and nobody else in our city has our phone number. (Explain area codes if asked, but don't have the child learn yours—he or she may dial it.)

Parents at work   Either have your child learn your work number(s) or post them by the phone where he or she can find them with the help of an adult. Explain how you ask for Mom and Dad at work ("Pam Smith," not "Mom").

About me   Teach your child his or her birthday, weight and height. Point out hair color and eye color, too.

3 ✻ BASIC MATERIALS, OR WHAT IS THAT STUFF?

The games here help your child to learn what common things are made of. Before teaching the composition of these items, make sure that he or she has a complete vocabulary for the common ones—chairs, brushes, overalls and so on (included in Chapter One: Basic Things).

Two of the basics   Lead your child around the house once for each of the following basic materials—*wood* and *plastic*. Find lots of examples of each and have the child handle them.

Then hold two scavenger hunts—one for the child to "find three wooden things" in a particular room, and the other (near a supply of toys) to "touch as many plastic things as you can before I finish counting to twenty."

The other three basics   As above, but introduce your child to the concepts of *metal, paper* and *cloth*. (A metal game with magnets, a bit more difficult, is found in Chapter Ten: Science Tricks.)

Medium hard I   As above, but concentrate on the kitchen and teach the materials found below. To avoid confusing your child and to reinforce basic concepts at the same time, use "double names" such as "wax paper" and "wax candles."

wax
bristles (on brushes)
stainless steel and/or silver
aluminum (foil, too)
cellophane (in different forms such as tape
    and food wrap)

Medium hard II   As above. Since some of these additional kitchen materials can be difficult, even for an adult, resort to approximations if necessary—for instance, "rubbery plastic" and "stiff plastic." Choose items from your own kitchen.

Clothing materials I   As above, but try to choose plain colors (patterns can be learned in game group 4):

cotton   cotton flannel
cotton denim   cotton canvas
cotton corduroy   cotton/synthetic
                          blend

Clothing materials II   As above, but with:

wool   wool/synthetic blend
suede   leather
velours   polyester, nylon,
                          etc. (or just
                          "synthetic
                          fabric")
. . . or whatever you have on hand.

What's jumping out of your closet?   Take turns with
your child, hiding in the child's closet or behind the
bureau. Fling out clothes, one item at a time. What
material is it?

Sink, dissolve or float   With your child, experiment
with which foods sink, float or dissolve in cups of water.
Nuts, marshmallows, popcorn, sugar, honey, raw rice
and fruit bits are good for a start.

Explain afterwards that if the object is heavier than
the water it is pushing out of the way, it will sink.
Otherwise it will float. If you like, the child can eat all the
evidence; or, for an older child, only the evidence for the
answers he or she guessed correctly.

4 ✳ BASIC PATTERNS AND DECORATIONS, OR
THAT CHAIR IS GOING WILD

These games help your child notice and identify basic
patterns, which aids both visual discrimination and vocabulary development. Look for patterns and decorations
like those below in your closets, on your furniture and, if
necessary, in magazine pictures. For a child under three
choose examples that differ quite clearly.

Clothing patterns   Take your child on a pattern tour of
the house (or even of a fabric store) or assemble, ahead
of time, patterns like the following to identify:

solid color	stripes	herringbone
plaid	polka dots	and just
checks	flowered	"patterned"
	pattern	

Then either mix them up and have your child identify

them, or ask the child to find other examples (if they are easily available).

Clothing decorations   As above, but with:

tassles	yarn-	ruffles
sequins	decorated	lace
smocking	embroidered	furry material
tucks		

Other patterns   Same as above, but with:

wood grain (or "wood pattern")
patterned linoleum
patterned carpet
paint texture
wallpaper patterns (perhaps floral or abstract)
a marble pattern

Finderino   Have your child lead you around the house, finding examples of as many of these patterns as possible.

5 ✳ COUNTING BY ROTE, OR WAY HIGH

Whether they have any understanding of numbers or not, most children love to count. Doing so is a good introduction to numbers. (These games build on the foundation provided in Chapter Three: Basic Concepts. And they are a preview to many more number games in Chapter Ten: Science Tricks and Chapter Twelve: Numbers.)

Getting up there   This game is one of the few that

cannot really be divided into five-minute subsections. Instead, repeat it several days in a row.

Begin by telling your child that the trick to counting "way up high" is knowing the "number families." All the numbers in the twenties family sound like two ("two-enty" or "twenty") and start with the number two. All the thirties family sound like three ("three-urty" or "thirty") and start with the number three.

Next write them down in family lines, with plenty of space between the numbers but with no confusing punctuation in between:

10	11	12	13	14	15	16	17	18	19
20	21	22	23	24	25	26	27	28	29
30	31	32	33	34	35	36	37	38	39
40	41	42	43	44	45	46	47	48	49
50	and so on up to 100								

Explain each family, what it sounds like and what it starts with, including the somewhat confusing tens family that sounds like "teen."

Next show your child—whether or not he or she can read numbers well—that each family has 1, 2, 3, 4, 5, 6, 7, 8 and 9 hidden inside it.

Then show that the families themselves go from the two, the twenties—to nine, the nineties.

When at least part of this is clear to your child, count along with him or her from 1 to 100. Point out each new family as you go and point out too, for example, that after the thirties family, that sound like *three,* comes the forties family, that sound like *four*—just like 4 comes after 3 in the little numbers.

Count it   Have your child review this counting, all the way to 100.

6 ✳ SPECIAL FACTS, OR HEARTS ARE FOR VALENTINE'S DAY

The games here teach your child a few of the many cultural celebrations on our calendar and what we are supposed to be celebrating on those days.

Fun holidays I   Help your child learn the name of each holiday, its date, its main purpose, its colors or decorations and its special food or activities, if any. Begin with:

> your two main religious holidays
> Independence Day
> Valentine's Day
> Halloween

Fun holidays II   Same as the above, but with:

> New Year's Day
> Memorial Day
> Labor Day
> Thanksgiving

Other fun days   As above, but with the birthdays of key family members.

7 ✳ WHAT DOES WHAT, OR THAT'S HOW A COOKIE CRUMBLES

These games explore and describe simple changes in things or materials. They will turn your kitchen into a junior chemistry lab, with enough action, in some cases, even for a toddler. Some of the slower experiments for older children can be begun in Mini-School one day and finished another day.

Remember to use words like "kid chemist" or "kid scientist" to get your child accustomed to the words and to the idea that science is fun. (More science games—some of them extensions of these—are found in Chapter Ten: Science Tricks.)

Watch it happen   Have your child observe, touch, stir, taste, or otherwise explore the following materials, before *and* after the action occurs:

> pudding thickens
> cookies crumble
> chalk or dirt washes away

Kitchen fun   As above, but with:

> cake ingredients mix into batter
> cake rises
> baking soda foams in water (and makes dough
>   or batter rise)

Almost magic   As above, but with:

> bread ingredients become dough
> bread rises in a warm place
> meat hardens when cooked

Do it yourself   As above, but with:

> eggs scramble
> paper crumples
> paper rips
> paper folds

Very elaborate   As above, but with:

cream whips into whipped cream
cream shakes into butter (if you really have
   about 45 minutes on a weekend day)

It rots I   As above, but set out a piece of banana, meat or other vestige of your child's meal in a moist place where no one will grab it. Tell your child that we are "junior scientists" about to study rotting and that you will help him or her start a "scientist's report." Have your child watch you write down a simple title, like "Report: Rotting," and the date.

It rots II   Then, in the next Mini-School, have the child check the rotting process. You should complete the report with something like "rotten by January 10th. Signed—Mom and Erik." (Your child will do more of the scientist's report in Chapter Ten: Science Tricks.)

It dries out   As above, including a report, but use a piece of bread, a leaf or other not-too-moist object.

It thaws or melts   As above, but set out an ice cube or other frozen item (inside or outside) and watch it thaw. Do your report.

It freezes   Put a small amount of water or fruit juice in a paper cup in the freezer. See what has happened by the end of the Mini-School session and by the next day's Mini-School. Don't forget your report. (You might also want to add an old popsicle stick in an hour or so if you have one. Presto—popsicle.)

It warms and cools   Put some warm water or hot chocolate on the stove and touch it occasionally (and safely) as it warms slowly.

Then let it cool, also touching it periodically.

Chapter Five: Pre-Reading

WHAT, WHY AND WHO

The learning games in this area will prepare your child for reading, making it easier for him or her to learn in later Mini-Schools with you, or when he or she goes to elementary school. Game groups focus on noticing small differences, distinguishing shapes, learning the alphabet, noticing pictures, moving from left to right and top to bottom in a book, following directions, learning the letter sounds, hearing rhymes, listening to alliterations, identifying letters, helping to invent a story and looking at familiar books and songs while you talk and sing along with your child. (More advanced games are in Chapter Fifteen: Reading.)

This kindergartenlike curriculum includes skills your child quite obviously needs, such as learning the alphabet, and others that many people take for granted and might forget to point out. For example, children need to be taught that we always read from left to right. And "b" and "d" also look very much alike to children, at least more similar than "A" and "a." These are distinctions that must also be learned.

With the foundation provided in all these games, your child may suddenly surprise you by begging to learn how to "really read." Or, of course, your child may be satisfied to learn later—but will enter kindergarten or first grade with an excellent background. In any event, be prepared!

Even a young baby can learn from some of these games, provided that no one expects him or her to chime in. Hearing the alphabet, letter sounds, rhymes and alliterations are all enjoyable for a baby and might make him or her more attuned to language.

A toddler will be intrigued with all these performances, too. He or she can also imitate the letter sounds, learn some letters and begin to follow directions and produce rhymes and alliterations.

A preschooler can learn to do all these games. With them, he or she will come to realize that letters and words are fun and will become familiar with handling books, too.

But remember that the best training for reading is not even listed here. It involves two key, non–Mini-School activities—reading to your child nearly every day, and building his or her spoken language skills through attentive conversation. It is also a good idea for the child to see his or her parents reading their own newspapers, magazines and books. Mention to your child, occasionally, something you have learned from your own reading. All these additional efforts will help motivate your child to learn to read and create the language background needed to do so.

In the regular game groups, easier activities precede harder ones, both within a game group and among them. Choose five minutes of activities for each Mini-School session.

1 ✳ Noticing Small Differences, or What's Going On Here?

The games here teach your child to pay attention to small differences and to remember what they are. This skill is useful in distinguishing among letters like "b," "d" and "p" and between similar words like "snake" and "smoke." It also makes everything around, from cloud patterns to wallpaper, a little bit more interesting.

What's up?   Before your child comes into the room for Mini-School, put a chair in an unusual place. Ask what is different.

Then ask the child to put his or her head down, hiding the eyes. Quickly change the position of two medium-sized objects (put a milk carton into the fruit bowl or the wastebasket in front of the TV, for example). Ask again, "What is different?"

Next change the position of smaller objects, placing them where they will be visible (such as a glass full of water in the middle of the kitchen floor). Ask "What's going on around here? What's different?"

Look hard   While your child is watching, line up three small familiar objects in front of him or her. Tell the child to look carefully and to remember what's there, because you will be taking one of them away soon. Remember to have your child name each object from left to right a couple of times, saying the names over to himself or herself. Tell your child this is a "memory trick."

Then ask your child to hide his or her eyes. Remove one object. Which is missing?

Look harder   As above, only use six objects. Remove one.

Look even harder   As above, only remove two objects at once, then three.

Look outside   Stand at the window or outside with your child. Ask him or her to tell you how two quite similar trees differ; how two similar clouds differ; how two squares of the sidewalk differ; or other small distinctions that can be made.

2 ✳ DIFFERENT SHAPES, OR BE A SHAPE DETECTIVE

These games bring your child one step closer to noticing the small differences among alphabet letters. (They provide exercises like those found on IQ and other standardized tests.) And they stress differences in size, shape, tilt, left vs. right side and other broad features—differences more important for distinguishing letters than, say, a smudge or a color difference.

One line at a time   Draw a line of triangles such as the following:

Then ask your child to be a "shape detective." Tell him or her to look hard at the first triangle, the one on the left. Now move along from left to right and point out which other triangles are *exactly* like the one on the left.

Do the same with a line of squares such as:

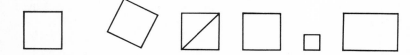

Remind the child that we go from left to right when we are shape detectives, because that's what big kids do when they read.

More shapes As above, only use circles and rectangles.

Which is different I? Stretch your own artistic abilities by drawing two to four lines of four familiar objects. Within a line, all are alike except one, which has something missing, such as:

Line by line, and looking left to right, ask your child which one is different. What is missing?

Which is different II?   As above, only with longer lines of objects and slightly more complicated ones—perhaps fancy flowers, one with its center missing, and dogs, with one missing an ear.

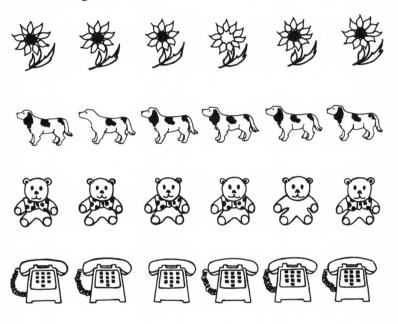

3 ✳ THE ALPHABET, OR ABC TRA-LA-LA

The games here are for teaching your child the alphabet. At this point they focus on the names, not the sounds, of the letters.

Sing it   Sing the "abc" song to your child until he or she can sing it all alone. Ours ended with ". . . now I know my ABCs. I'm as proud as I can be," or ". . . now I know my alphabet. I'm as proud as I can get."

Review it   Using a child's alphabet book of any kind, point to each letter as you sing, just to give the child a preliminary idea of its appearance. But review the song until it is "second nature" to the child before proceeding any farther.

Each letter I   Using a child's alphabet book that includes both "uppercase" and "lowercase" letters, help your child reach a basic recognition of letters Aa through Hh.

Each letter II   As above, but review Aa through Hh and add Ii through Pp.

Each letter III   As above, but review Aa through Pp and add Qq through Zz.

Each letter IV   Do a complete Aa through Zz review of both upper- and lowercase letters, in order. Then take turns, with your child turning to pages at random. Ask the child which letter is which. Repeat these games, on and off, until the child is almost "letter perfect."

4 ✳ FIND THE PICTURE, OR BE A PICTURE DETECTIVE

These games are designed to help your child notice and remember reasonably detailed visual information within books. They should also encourage your child's love of books.

Find it   Choose a short book, familiar to your child, that contains easy-to-turn pages and pictures of large objects such as a barn to illustrate some of the letters of the alphabet. (An alphabet book might be good here again, since they tend not to duplicate pictures.)

Tell your child to find a picture of, for example, a barn. Show him or her how to look on each page, from the beginning or front of the book to the end of the book. Be a "picture detective."

Find it (trickier)   Ask your child to find a more specific picture among similar ones. For example, if the book is about squirrels, ask the child to find one where the squirrel is sitting on the ground.

Find it (even trickier)   With a familiar book, teach your child how to "page through" a book quickly or "spot check" in areas of the book where he or she thinks a specific picture might be located.

5 ✳ LEFT TO RIGHT AND TOP TO BOTTOM, OR FOLLOW THE PATH THROUGH THE BOOK

This game will teach your child how books are read in Western culture, a method which is in no way obvious to a young citizen. Remind the child of this "book-path" while reading to him or her, too.

The path   Show your child the first word on the first page of a fairly short book. With your hand over his or her finger, sweep quickly along the first line of words, then the second and so on. Turn to a new page and ask the child which word comes first. Proceed through the book quickly. And stress to the child that we won't point to the words once we learn how to read (this habit slows the reading of many children).

6 ✳ FOLLOWING DIRECTIONS, OR LISTEN AND DO

The games here will sharpen your child's listening skills, memory and ability to follow directions. All of these are valuable for reading and school tasks in general. In fact, many kindergarten teachers might consider them the most important games in this Mini-School area!

Clap your hands   Tell your child to be absolutely quiet and look at "the teacher" because he or she will be asked to do two tricks. Emphasize that the child must listen carefully, do them in order and not begin until you are finished talking.

Start with one like "clap your hands, then scratch your tummy." Then do a few more two-part tricks such as:

jump twice, then touch the table
rub your tummy, then stamp your foot
fold your arms, then pat your head

Harder   As above, only progress to three-part and even four-part tricks. Teach your child to repeat the instructions to himself or herself as you say them, before beginning. By putting an activity into words we can remember it better.

Freeze   Sing or play some music while your child dances around. Tell him or her to stop fast or "freeze" as soon as the song stops. Do this several times.

"Simon Says"   Teach your child the rules—do what Simon says, one thing at a time, but *only* when "the teacher" actually says, "Simon says," first.

Start with, "Simon says pat your knees." "Simon says

scratch your ear," and so on. Then, "Touch your cheek"—oops!

Next give your child a turn to tell you what to do (whether or not he or she actually ever skips the "Simon Says" preface!)

7 ✳ LETTER SOUNDS, OR Z GOES ZZZZ

These games proceed beyond the names of the letters to their sounds, the important next step for future readers. If your child learns these sounds first, then applies that knowledge with your help, he or she will probably have a better chance of becoming a good speller later, too. These games also provide good practice in concentration.

The vowels　　Teach your child that the vowels in our alphabet are "a, e, i, o, u and sometimes y." Every word in every book and every word we say has one or more of these vowels in it—that's why we learn them first. Make up a little chant to do so.

Vowel sounds　　Teach your child what "the vowels say." Review these periodically. Tell your child "the vowel trick"—long "a" says its own name and so on. "A" is the hardest:

> long "a" says "a" as in snake and table
> short "a" says "a" as in fat and bath
> broad "a" says "aw" as in ball and wall

Next "E":

> long "e" says "e" as in we
> short "e" says "eh" as in bed

Next "I":

> long "i" says "i" as in ice cream
> short "i" says "ih" as in icky

Next "O":

> long "o" says "o" as in rope
> short "o" says "ah" as in mop

Next "U":

> long "u" says "u" as in usually
> short "u" says "uh" as in up

Next "Y":

> long "y" says "yuh" as in yogurt
> short "y" says "ee" as in happy

Some consonants I   Tell your child that these are much easier than the vowels because only two of them have more than one sound. An older child can, in each case, think of another word that uses that sound, too.

> "b" says "buh" as in ball
> "c" says two things—hard "c" says "kuh" as in cookie, and soft "c" says "suh" as in city
> "d" says "duh" as in Dad
> "f" says "fuh" as in fun
> "g" says two things—hard "g" says "guh" as in giggle, and soft "g" says "juh" as in George

Some consonants II   As above, but with these letters:

"h" says "huh" as in honey
"j" says "juh" as in jump
"k" says "kuh" as in kind
"l" says "luh" as in love
"m" says "muh" as in Mom
"n" says "nuh" as in no
"p" says "puh" as in puppy
"q" says "quuh" as in quack

Some consonants III   As above, but with these letters:

"r" says "ruh" as in run
"s" says "suh" as in snake
"t" says "tuh" as in tummy
"v" says "vuh" as in violet
"w" says "wuh" as in water
"x" says "cks" as in wax
"z" says "zuh" as in zebra

Alphabet sound review   Go over all the letter sounds, from A to Z.

Sounds in reverse I   Ask your child to help you put letters together to make words. (But don't expect him or her to synthesize the individual sounds into words at this point.)

Begin with the word "hat," asking your child what letter makes the "huh" sound. Write down the "h." Then ask what letter makes the "a" sound and write it down. And what letter makes the "tuh" sound. You write it down again. You and your child have just spelled out a word!

Now ask your "helper speller" to help you with:

bat	cat
rat	mat
sat	pat
fat	vat

Sounds in reverse II   As above, but with:

bet	get
let	met
net	pet
set	wet

Sounds in reverse III   As above, but with:

mop	cop
stop	lop
hop	pop
bop	top

Sounds in reverse IV   As above, but with:

bit	pit
hit	sit
lit	wit
mitt	slit

Sounds in reverse V   As above, but with the following.
(More reading games dealing with consonant and vowel
sounds are found in Chapter Fifteen: Reading.)

up	pup
cup	

. . . and review whichever ones from the previous games the child found to be hard.

Spell your name   As above, but with your child's name. If the spelling is irregular, just *tell* the child the next letter. Add a comment like, "Spelling is really weird sometimes. That's why you have me to help you. Some words can be hard even for adults."

8 ✻ RHYMES, OR ARE YOU A FUNNY BUNNY?

Babies will love to hear *you* play this game (announce, "I'm going to say some rhymes now."). And older children can play it with you, increasing their knowledge of words and word sounds.

Rhymes with I   Explain to your child that two words rhyme if they both end in the same sound. For example, "see" and "we" rhyme. Then ask your child to think of as many words as possible that rhyme with each of the words listed below. If the child gets stuck, give an easy hint such as (for "see") "it's in the middle of your leg."
    Accept anything that's a real word. If you get "clee," just tell your child that "clee" *does* rhyme with "see" and it *could* be a word in another language, but it isn't one in our language, so he or she should think of another one.
    Start with:

bat	up
met	bee
hop	four
sit	book

Rhymes with II   As above, but with:

pot	ten
slow	bar
four	bed
date	chair

Rhymes with III   As above, but with:

nail	town
gun	eye
fix	floor
write	toy

Rhyming harder   Ask your child to start the game by providing a word to rhyme. Then take turns saying rhyming words as long as you can.

9 ✳ ALLITERATIONS, OR THE BEGINNING SOUNDS THE SAME

Like rhymes, alliterations are fun for babies to hear. Older children can provide them by the copious cartful. They teach sound and word familiarity as well as a little concentration. (More games on alliterations are found in Family Chapter Twenty-One: Say a Poem.)

Duh, duh, duh and so on   Explain to your child that an alliteration is any two words—or more—that start with the same sound, the way "dog" and "dark" start with the "duh" or "d" sound.

With alliterations, no one cares how they are spelled—"cuckoo" and "kind" form an alliteration. But in these cases, point out the difference to your child.

Take turns with your child thinking of words that form alliterations with:

ball   monkey
cup   puppy
donkey   nope

A silly story   Ask your child to make up a silly story with as much alliteration as possible. Get the child started on:

a "fuh" story
a "ruh" story
a "muh" story

10 ✴ IDENTIFY LETTERS, OR PICK THE TRICKY

These games will help your child distinguish the differences among the tricky letters, those most likely to be confused. Before you begin, quickly review with the child all the written upper- and lowercase letters, Aa through Zz. Then focus on the pairs which follow. Remember to come back to these games periodically— these differences are readily forgotten.

Tricky I   Ask your child to identify the following letters and numbers in pairs:

"b" and "d" (the "b" has a belly on the right)
"b" and "p" (the "p" hangs down below the
    line like a puppy's tail)
"a" and "q" (the "q" is a quail with a long
    tail)

"g" and "q" (the "g" could reach up and grab
   its own goofy face)
"l" and "i" (the "i" has a dot for its hat)

Then write down the words "bed," "bop," "quack,"
"quagmire" and "lit," and ask your child to identify the
letters again.

Tricky II   As above, but with:

"q" and "p" (the "p" is pushing towards the
   rest of its word)
"3" and "E" (the "E" is pointing towards the
   rest of its word)
"6" and "e" (the "e" has a higher tummy)

For review, write down "quip," "3 Easters" and "6
eagles."

Tricky III   As above, but with the letters *your* child
has trouble distinguishing.

11 ✳ FILL IN THE BLANKS, OR HELP ME MAKE UP
A STORY

This game will reinforce, for your child, word sounds
and word sense (or nonsense) in the context of an oral
story. (A written version of this game is found in Chapter
Six: Pre-Writing, and more purely creative versions are
found in Chapter Nineteen: Story Recipes and Chapter
Twenty-Six: Make a Family Book.)

Our story   You begin a simple story, asking your child to listen to the sound hints and chime in with the missing words, as in the following example:

> "One morning a little girl woke up. She went downstairs to eat her b____ ('breakfast' or 'bread' or whatever). She drank some j____ ('juice,' etc.), and so on.

The stories can be easy or hard, short or long and as sensible or nonsensical as you like.

12 ✹ WORDS YOU KNOW, OR FOLLOW ALONG

This game will get your child accustomed to looking at groups of real words in print. This helps build the confidence needed to take the jump to real reading in later Mini-Schools or in regular school.

A short book we know   Choose a short and familiar book, one your child knows virtually by heart. You start reading it, pointing to each word. Then let the child continue to say the words alone, with an occasional boost from you. As he or she goes along, you point to each familiar word the child is reeling off. (Say something like, "When you learn how to read later, you'll know how to do this with any book. It will be a lot of fun.")

Songs we know   Use a familiar children's record that includes the written lyrics or write down the words to a familiar song yourself. As in the game above, help the child look at the words as you both sing.

Chapter Six: Pre-Writing

WHAT, WHY AND WHO

The learning games in this area are designed to provide the foundation for later writing skills. They include—holding the writing implement, understanding that writing is fun and important, touching the letters, developing small muscles and better eye-hand coordination, drawing with precision, connecting the dots to make letters and writing a story. These skills should be well in place before starting your child on the games in Chapter Thirteen: Writing.

The solid background here should increase your child's confidence so that he or she can jump right into writing in later Mini-Schools with you or get off to an excellent start in kindergarten or first grade. Make sure, also, to tell your child how you and your spouse use writing at home and at work. Encourage the grandparents to write postcards to the child, too.

The age at which to begin these games varies considerably from child to child, perhaps more than in most of the learning game areas. When little Erin, the child of a friend of mine, was two and a half, she had strong enough finger muscles and eye-hand coordination to sew beautifully with a regular needle. (My children could not. In fact, their reading skills were generally ahead of their writing skills until the two equalized at about age four.) It's safe to say, though, that these games are for preschoolers, but not for babies or even toddlers (except for the first one or two game groups).

1 ❋ WRITING IMPLEMENTS, OR HOLD IT, IT'S YOURS

This game teaches your child how to hold a writing implement. Practicing the right way strengthens the proper writing muscles; practicing the wrong way does not. You should, in fact, gradually encourage your preschooler to hold even crayons in the proper fashion.

Let your child make his or her own writing practice kit, choosing one crayon, one pencil, one ball-point pen and one felt-tipped pen. Put them in a special place, so that your child can choose one writing implement for each game in this Mini-School area. (If the game seems a bit hard, suggest the felt-tipped pen. It is probably the easiest to move across the page.)

The "tiny person" and the bracer Show your child how to hold the implement between the thumb and forefinger, with the little finger resting on the paper. Allow the "tail" of the implement to reach up high so that a "tiny person" can perch up there for a ride. The other hand should lie down on the paper near the top, bracing it so that it doesn't slide around. We call that hand the "bracer."

Then ask your child to make broad sweeping strokes all around the paper. Have him or her drop the implement periodically. That way the child's muscles can rest, and you can review again with him or her how to hold it.

2 ✳ Writing Is Fun and Important, or Dear Grandma and Grandpa

These games suggest to your child some of the reasons we write—to remember things, to tell things to other people, to have fun and to be nice.

Why I write   Bring home some of the writing that you and your spouse do at work. Also assemble your checkbook records, grocery and other lists and the like. Show them and read parts of them to your child. Stress why you wrote it all down and why you are glad you did.

Dictate a letter   Ask your child who he or she would like to write a letter to, with your help. It may be a grandparent, Mr. Rogers, Kermit the Frog, Richard Scarry or Santa Claus.

Then show your child how to begin with "Dear ——." Remind him or her not to talk *too* quickly because you are going to write it all down. Do so, *exactly,* and read it back to the child.

Next the child may draw a quick picture in the corner and lick the stamp. You do the envelope, and off it goes. (Don't get the child's hopes up ahead of time, but we have found that many TV personalities will write back.)

Dictate a story   Ask your child to tell you a story about anything. It might be about a monster, about what happened yesterday at preschool, or about the time a sibling was "mean." Write down *exactly* what the child says, about one sentence per page. Then, as you read it back, the child can illustrate it. (A book like this would make a wonderful present.)

"Cave kid" writing   If you happen to have a piece of charcoal and a white rock around, this is a fun learning game.

Tell your child that this is the way kids wrote in the "cave days," before paper and pencils were invented. Then let the child mark on the rock (not too far from some cleanup supplies).

3 ✳ THE TACTILE SENSE, OR FEEL THE LETTERS

This game acknowledges the fact that some children learn best when they can touch the objects they are learning about. It seems to make abstract concepts more concrete.

Touch it   Assemble or make some touchable letters. (Use alphabet blocks with raised letters. Draw letters on the sidewalk with chalk. Or line up pebbles, sticks and acorns to make a few of the letters. Or do a combination of all three.)

Then hold your hand over your child's index finger and help him or her move it along the outline of the letters. Say each one as you go along.

4 ✳ SMALL MUSCLES AND EYE-HAND PRACTICE, OR FINGERS, FINGERS

These activities, some of which might seem quite far from writing, are designed to train the small muscles needed to propel pencil across paper and to accustom the eye and hand to cooperate on small-scale projects. Some tasks are more difficult than you might imagine. They need not be done with full proficiency before proceeding to later games or mini-school areas. (More games on the

practical uses of these activities are found in Chapter
Seven: Daily Life.)

Try it I   If you have the supplies, have the child spend
a few minutes on projects like the following:

> attaching small lego blocks together
> threading beads onto stiff string or yarn

Try it II   As above, but with:

> snapping a snap
> zipping a zipper
> lacing (not tying) a shoe
> buttoning a sweater

Try it III   As above, but with:

> folding a paper napkin into a rectangle, a
>   square and a triangle
> cutting out large simple shapes that you have
>   drawn for your child

Try it IV   As above, but have your child sew with a
pre-threaded, pre-knotted needle.

5 ✳ PRECISION DRAWING, OR HANG ON TO THAT
FELT-TIPPER

These games, like game groups 1 and 2 in Chapter
Five: Pre-Reading, are designed to draw your child's
attention to the details necessary for distinguishing and
making letters. They extend the small muscle and eye-
hand coordination practice of the previous game group
and apply it more directly to writing.

Coloring books   Ask your child to color inside the lines of various pictures (holding the writing implement properly). This is probably the best occasional use of coloring books.

Draw shapes   Have your child draw a large circle, then a square, then a rectangle, then a triangle and then several long horizontal lines. If necessary, you can draw them first in light pencil and ask him or her to follow your lines.

What's missing?   Begin by making a simple incomplete drawing yourself, asking your child what is missing. Then have your child draw in that missing feature (other "missing drawings" are found in Chapter Five: Pre-Reading). Try the following:

    a face with no eyes
    a head with only one ear
    a square with one open side
    a circle with a gap
    a chair with one leg missing
    a TV with no dials
    a door with no doorknob

Color-in letters   Draw big, thick letters, especially the ones that seem hard for your child. Then have him or her color them in, reviewing their names and sounds at the same time.

6 ✳ CONNECT THE DOTS, OR YOU DID IT

These games are "almost-writing," and a child who can do them should feel very proud. They provide the muscle practice and eye-hand skills and review the letter shapes necessary for writing.

Connect a name   Show your child first what you mean by connecting the dots. In each case, make sure that he or she starts where you would if you were making the letter.

Connect all the letters I   Apart from the excitement of your child's name, some letters are easier to write than others. Using connect-the-dots, begin with these easier ones among the uppercase letters: A, C, D, E, F, H, I. Draw the dots for the child to connect in each case, one by one.

Connect all the letters II   As above, with more of the easier uppercase letters to create: K, L, O, P, T and V.

Connect all the letters III   As above, but now do the dots for some of the more difficult uppercase letters: B, G, M, N, Q, R.

Connect all the letters IV   As above, but now finish the harder uppercase letters: S, U, W, X, Y, Z.

Connect all the letters V   Next begin with some of the easier lowercase letters, still with dots: b, c, d, h, i and l.

Connect all the letters VI   As above, but with the rest of the easier lowercase letters: o, p, r, t, v.

Connect all the letters VII   As above, but with more of the lowercase letters: a, e, f, g, j.

Connect all the letters VIII   As above, but with more of the lowercase letters: k, m, n, q, s.

Connect all the letters IX   Finish the rest of the lowercase letters: u, w, x, y and z.

Letter review   With the connect-the-dots method, review all of the letters periodically.

7 ✸ FILL IN THE BLANKS, OR HELP ME WRITE A STORY

In these games, your child can put his or her "almost-writing" into practice and see the beautiful results of all that detailed learning. The next step after this one is real writing. (Creative story writing comes in Chapter Nineteen: Story Recipes and Chapter Twenty-Six: Make a Family Book.)

You write I   Help your child get started by having him or her dictate a simple story to you. (It could be about plans for a birthday party, what we could do Saturday morning or what it's like in my favorite imaginary bedroom.)

You write most of it down, but leave a blank for three or four of the key short words. Then make the dots so that your child can "almost write" those words, one by one. Presto—a story.

You write II   As above, but with a different story, and with the child helping you to spell the missing words. (Surprisingly, children who know their word sounds well can sometimes spell better than they can read.)

You write III   As above, but with a different story and with the child actually writing, without dots, a couple of the letters in the missing words.

Chapter Seven: Daily Life

The learning games in this area are a potpourri of skills and understandings that your child can use in daily life. They cover a wide range, including how to water plants, how to match colors by memory, how to understand basic traffic rules, how the toaster works. They fall into the categories of home management, observing things, sequences, how appliances work and advanced skills.

Many of these skills will build pride in your child, the kind of pride that can be felt every day when he or she sets the table or makes a bed. Contributing to the necessary and important work at home makes a child feel responsible, too, as though he or she were "big like Mom and Dad." (This is the way children must have felt on our great-grandparents' and grandparents' farms, where daily chores probably also led to a sense of family solidarity.)

Activities like some of these are also taught in the Montessori method. It has been demonstrated that children can accomplish a great deal if they are taught how to—and if you realize that it will be more work for you at the very beginning, while you are still monitoring their chores. Some early cultures were experts in this, too—in parts of Africa preschoolers get up, start the fire and take tea to their parents in bed!

Of course, this section isn't all servitude, nor am I recommending anything that is dangerous. Many of the games use daily activities to lay the groundwork for logical thinking—a capacity not fully developed until the teenage years, psychologists tell us. Other games teach familiarity with the daily features of our world.

Toddlers can do a few of the activities here, but most of this area is for preschoolers.

Remember that the games and game groups get harder (generally) as you proceed through the chapter. Choose five minutes of activities for each Mini-School session.

1 ✳ HOME MANAGEMENT, OR WHAT WE NEED TO DO AROUND HERE

These games will give your child a sense of accomplishment and you a little help—provided that you teach them step by step and avoid nagging. (There's no time like the present to show your child that we all help around the house, too.)

Once your child can perform a given task regularly and without any supervision, you might want to award a small prize (a piece of candy, a nickel, a chance to stay up five minutes later or the like). This will build an association between work and reward that you may want to invoke later if you plan to pay your child an allowance.

But whether you reward your child tangibly or not, remember to stress that the child is doing these projects because he or she is big now, can help with what needs to be done and is responsible enough to do the tasks alone. If you also present them as fun, they will be considered fun.

One last word of warning—avoid a sexist division of labor now and you won't see so much of it later.

Set a table   Show your child where the family's forks, spoons and knives are kept. Have him or her count out the right number for the whole family. Show where people will sit. Then explain how the fork goes on the left and the knife and spoon on the right. (Make up a little chant or song.)

Pouring   This can be taught even to a toddler, if you use water on a low table. It helps develop eye-hand coordination. Set out a measuring cup or other small-spouted pitcher and a wide-mouthed glass. Show your child exactly where the water is supposed to come out and just how far to tip the pitcher, using one hand on the handle and the other on the bottom.

Progress, with older children, to pouring cereal or raw rice for fun; then, later, juice and milk for meals. The pleasantly presented ground rule is that the child cleans up any puddles.

Watering plants   Show your child how to fill the watering can; how to carry it, level, with one hand underneath and one hand on the handle; how to pour with one hand on the handle and the other still underneath; and how to mop up a puddle if it occurs. Even a three-year-old can learn how much water to give each of several of the family's plants.

The first time your child does it, your hand should be over his or hers. The second time you should only check the amount of water. After that, those plants are his or her responsibility. All you need to do is to say, every Sunday morning or whenever, "It's plant time." (Teach the names of the plants as you go along, too.) Once you have given your child the responsibility, don't check his or her work.

Stirring   Stirring ingredients together takes coordination and provides help for you. Tell your child to keep the spoon low. And point out the one-quarter, one-half and three-quarter cup marks as you go along. (See Chapter Ten: Science Tricks, for preliminary games on fractions.)

Emptying wastebaskets and processing recycling   Assign several feasible wastebaskets to your child on a twice-a-week schedule. Give the child an empty grocery bag and show him or her exactly how to dump the wastebasket's contents into it. Stress that we all drop a little trash now and then—we just pick it up afterwards. If you separate articles for recycling, teach your child how to identify those materials and put them in a special place.

Teach the technique once, watch your child do it the next time, and after that only announce, "It's trash time." (And remember not to put bare razor blades or other dangerous items in the wastebaskets.)

Dusting   Assign your child a small room. Teach him or her how to use the dustcloth, what *not* to dust and how to go around the room in a circle to avoid omission or repetition. You accompany your child the first time and inspect it afterwards the second time; after that the room is the child's responsibility.

Making a bed   Teach your child how to pull up the sheet and blanket, tuck them in around the edges, smooth the top and then fold on the spread. This is quite difficult and, if you have really hurried mornings, don't make it a regular chore until your child is four or five years old.

Washing dishes   This is not as difficult as you might think, and children seem to love playing with water anyway. Show your child how to carry a stool or chair over to the sink, so that he or she will be tall enough to perform this task. Make sure the dishes are reachable. Then, depending on the age of the child, you may or may not have to turn the water on and adjust the temperature. Next show him or her how to drizzle the soap onto the soap pad. Then demonstrate, with your hand over the child's, how to scrub a plate, a glass, a cup and utensils. Show the child how to rinse without flooding the kitchen floor. Next you inspect each dish and you or the child can put them in the dish rack. (This isn't as hard as it sounds, but we don't do it every day either!)

Operating household appliances   A preschooler can be taught how to operate appliances such as a toaster and a "hokey" (one of those small, cordless vacuum cleaners that picks up the child's dinner crumbs from any surface and even does a creditable job on the child's bedroom carpet). Mine even argue over who "gets to hokey" first.

Again, follow the principle of demonstrating it step by step, with your hands over the child's, then one supervision, then deed over the responsibility.

Look around your house for other appliances that your child might be able to cope with easily.

Answering the telephone (professionally)   Teach your child how to pick up the receiver, say "hello" loudly enough, listen, set the receiver down gently on the table and go to get whomever the call is for *or,* in the case of a problem, an adult. Depending on your child's age and your child-care arrangements, you might need to give the child a standard answer for use when the parent is not there.

Dialing the telephone   This is harder. First you have to pick up the receiver, listen for the dial tone, dial each number solidly to the bar and listen for the rings and the "hello." Practice with the weather number or another recording. When it's learned, call someone special.

Chore list   With your child, make a master list of household chores. The child may now sign up for the ones he or she can accomplish.

Household floor plan   This is not really work but orientation and spatial thinking, though it relates to the home. Draw a large square or rectangle on a piece of paper to indicate the ground floor of your house or apartment. Mark the front door and other doors and draw the nearby street(s).

Ask your child to find the location of the living room on the floor plan. Help him or her mark it "LR." Then do the other main rooms. Next, have your child draw little squares for the main windows, too. Then block out the other floors, if you have any.

While completing the floor plan, help your child conceptualize it all by giving hints such as "what's over the kitchen?" or "what's in between the kitchen and the living room?"

Manners   To cut down on the nagging problem of teaching manners only when you see *bad* manners, make a list with your child of what we don't do—"no stamping on the floor at mealtime," for example. Then ask the

child if he or she knows *why* that isn't good to do.
Provide your own rationale, too. And post the complete
list for handy reference!

2 ✳ PRE-LOGIC, OR OBSERVING THINGS

Being able to observe small differences and match
items mentally to others you have seen is one foundation
for later logical thinking. It also helps in daily life and
makes the world a lot more interesting. A toddler can do
the simple versions of some of these games.

Pairs   Assemble a group of four to twelve small
objects that form two to six pairs. (The number depends
on the age of the child.) These could be spoons, blocks
and spools of colored thread. Then ask your child to "put
them in pairs, with the two that are alike going together."

Pairs II   Once your child can sort many pairs quickly,
put half of them—a complete set of unpaired objects—in
one room and the other set in another room. Ask your
child to choose one item (perhaps, a spool of blue
thread), pick it up, say its name to himself or herself, put
it back down and get its pair in the other room.

This trains your child's memory, especially when the
child can do it "in triples," fetching three objects at once
to put in their groups.

Differences   Outdoors, ask your child to find:

> six (or more) leaves in *different* shades of
> green
> six (or more) pebbles that have different
> patterns or are different sizes

six (or more) sticks of different lengths
six (or more) different flowers

Grocery differences   On a grocery-shopping trip, teach
your child differences (and the new words to go with
them) such as these:

one-half gallon of milk vs. one quart of milk
one dozen eggs vs. one-half dozen eggs
one pound of carrots vs. two pounds of
    carrots
a three-pound roast vs. a ten-pound roast
a one-pound box of crackers vs. a one-half-
    pound box
a six-roll package of toilet paper vs. a four-roll
    package

3 ✳ SEQUENCES, OR WHAT'S NEXT?

These games draw your child's attention to the order
in which tasks are performed, another early basis for later
logical thinking.

Your own order   Ask your child what gets put on first
when he or she gets dressed. What comes next? Go
through the whole sequence.

Then ask which meal we eat in the morning? Which
one in the evening?

Next ask your child about the pre-bedtime sequence
of activities.

Other sequences   Make or buy sets of large picture
cards, with each set showing different stages of a simple
action or story. In one set, the first card could show a

seed, the next a seedling, then a sapling, then a tree. Another sequence might show a snow storm piling up snow around a bush.

Shuffle the cards within a sequence, then ask your child to arrange them in the proper order. (Remember, even for practice here, that stories go from left to right. This habit is a very important one to build in pre-readers.)

Draw it   Ask your child to draw three different pictures of absolutely anything. Then have him or her tell you a story using the first one, then the second one, then the third.

If the child is old enough, shuffle these pictures, lay them out again from left to right and ask the child to tell you a whole new story in *that* order, however surrealistic.

4   ✳   HOW HOME APPLIANCES WORK, OR IS THAT OUR REFRIGERATOR HUMMING?

This game is designed to give your child a basic idea of how household appliances work. "Basic" means, "The toaster has a hiding place for the piece of bread. When you push the bread down, coils next to it get hot and they burn the bread a tiny bit. We don't put our fingers in because we don't want to eat burnt fingers for breakfast." (More games involving household appliances are found in Chapter Fourteen: Fun Facts and How to Find Them.)

The idea is to pique your child's curiosity about all the seemingly ordinary items in our daily lives. It is also to suggest to your child that appliances are not magical or demonic. (Your child may have small fears here that you can easily discover and then allay by asking if the child "likes the toaster" or other appliance.)

How it works   Ask your child to lead you around the house to "our household appliances" and you will tell him or her a little bit about how each one works. Get the child started with a short definition of an appliance. Turn each one on. And stress that he or she might want to invent an appliance someday. (You'll soon know that I'm not a mechanical engineer, but start with ones like the following.)

> The vacuum cleaner. It sucks air and dirt into a place where there is no air. But it could *never* suck up a child.

> The toilet. Water washes the body wastes down into sewage pipes under the street. These pipes are connected to every house. They take everybody's wastes to a sewage treatment plant.

> The stove. If it is electric, electricity comes into the electric plugs through big wires outside the house. When the stove is plugged in, this electricity makes the coils on top of the stove and in the oven warm up to cook our food. If it's gas, the gas comes in through pipelines attached to the house and burns by itself under the burners on top of the stove.

> The refrigerator. Freon runs through tubes inside it and cools the air to keep our food from rotting.

> The car. Gasoline from the gas station goes into the motor, which makes parts of it move around. It is attached to the wheels and makes them move around, too. That's how we're able to go.

The TV. Sound waves and light waves come
into it from the TV station where the
programs are acted out. The waves are
too tiny for us to see. They jiggle up the
inside of the TV set and make it put out
pictures and sounds. The people are not
inside the TV. They are at the TV station
acting out pretend stories.

5 ✹ ADVANCED SKILLS, OR STOP SIGNS AND LEFT
AND RIGHT

The games in this series are becoming more advanced.
Once your child understands them, he or she will be a
real junior citizen, at home in the world.

Mailing things   Begin by showing your child how to
stick a stamp on an envelope. Once he or she can write
well enough, have him or her address it, too, down to the
zip code. Then take it to the post office and put it in the
mailing slot. While you're there, point out the scales used
for weighing packages, the bins where they are held, the
"dollies" used to load them into the trucks, the slots
where the mail carriers get the mail to take to everybody's houses, the trucks to take other mail to nearby
cities or to the airport and so on. Ask your child why he
or she thinks we need post offices.

Just the facts   Make sure your child remembers his or
her address and phone number (part of Chapter Four:
Basic Knowledge). Then teach the name of your neighborhood, the community or city, county, state and
country. Put them together into a giant address!

Traffic rules   As your child learns to read traffic signs (see Chapter Fifteen: Reading), teach him or her some basic traffic rules:

stop on red	go on green
slow on yellow	slow on flashing
stop for stop signs	yellow
yield (let the other cars go first)	slow down for curves
left turn has to wait until other cars are out of the way	speed limits in various places

Construction   Take your child to a nearby construction site and show him or her the "excavation to make the basement" and as many as possible of the following:

the steel girders	the wooden scaffolding
welders	the cement mixers
masons	the electric wiring
electricians	the sewage pipes
the clean water pipes	
plumbers	

Left and right   Make sure your child knows the difference between his or her right hand ("the one you *write* with?") and his or her left hand. Then teach the right arm, right leg and so on, as opposed to those on the left side. Next quiz the child by saying "look to your right." Remember to emphasize that this statement means "look toward the right side of your body."

Tying shoes   This is a task for a four- or five-year-old. Depending upon your child's dexterity, you may want to teach it in stages and only for part of a Mini-School session. Have your child wear shoes with long laces.

Squat behind the child so that your hands are where the child's hands would be. Break the task into parts, showing:

the initial tie
the first loop to pinch
over the "pointer" finger or the thumb
the shoving under, inside the loop
the final tug

Ask the child to do one part at a time, then finally put them all together.

Chapter Eight: Visual Information

The learning games in this area are designed to help your child learn some of the basic conventions or "tricks" used in presenting visual information. The games cover key visual tricks found in books, on TV, in magazines and on maps and globes. They also help your child learn common visual symbols and some of the wondrous things our eyes can't see at all.

Unless your child is told, how would he or she ever guess that a "cartoon balloon" attached to someone's mouth means that person is saying those words? Or that TV can emphasize a scene through a "freeze frame," holding our attention on a specific camera shot? Or why north should always be at the top of a map? Or a heart symbolize love?

In a visual culture such as ours, such conventions are nearly as important to understand as knowing that we read from left to right. Yet, your child's "visual literacy" may be no farther advanced than his or her "word literacy." Many children point to a picture in a book and ask, "Why is that house *over* that kid?"—when the house is drawn higher on the page to indicate that it is *behind* the person.

These games will teach even an older baby a few of

the visual tricks. (Try the "whistle marks" or other simple ones.)

Toddlers and preschoolers may also be taught several of them in a group in Mini-School, by paging through a few Walt Disney books, for example, or others.

Remember that activities within each game tend to progress from the easier to the harder, as do the game groups themselves. Find five minutes worth of activities.

1 ✳ BOOK TRICKS, OR IS DONALD DUCK WHISTLING IN THAT PICTURE?

When you play these games with your child, you may be surprised to find that book pictures can be puzzling. For example, the methods used to show a character singing or thinking may seem confusing until one recognizes the techniques used. Once you explain a trick, ask your child why he or she thinks it is needed. Then stress that books can only use flat pictures. We can't hear or touch the people in books; we can only see them. (Try to pique your child's curiosity about different styles of book illustration, too, as you go along.)

Tricks I   Find and explain these common visual tricks in your child's books. After going over each one, have your child do as many of the actions as are possible in front of the mirror to see whether or not the specific trick seems reasonable.

> whistling (small round mouth, lines splaying
>   out from it)
> singing (larger round or oval-shaped mouth,
>   with or without musical notes nearby)
> shouting or yelling (mouth wide open, with or
>   without wider lines around it)

sleeping or snoring (curved eye lines, with or
without a pile of "Zzzz's" nearby)

talking (words in a cartoon balloon attached
to the person talking by a short line or
hook)

thinking (words or pictures in a cartoon
balloon connected by bubbles to the person thinking)

Tricks II   As above, but with:

worried (lines on the forehead)

mad or mean (face squunched up tightly)

curious or surprised (eyebrows pointing up in
the middle)

jumping or running (lines behind a person,
showing where he or she came from)

confusion (sometimes an overlap or collage
effect)

behind something (drawn above it)

loud talking (uppercase or big letters)

quiet talking (tiny letters)

listening or hearing (widening concentric circles proceeding from the ear)

hollering or shouting ("eeeyyooo!" or equiv-
alent word)

rain (slanted lines or pear-shaped drops)

2 ✳ TV TRICKS, OR WHY IS THAT PICTURE
STUCK?

The games here can make your child become more
curious about what he or she takes for granted on TV.
This is the one group of games that can be done while

watching *Sesame Street, Electric Company* or a similarly inventive show.

TV gimmicks   Show and explain to your child:

> freeze frame—to emphasize one picture (it stalls)
>
> dissolve—to show a transition or change from one scene to another (one picture seems to melt into the other)
>
> split screen—to show two different pictures at once (there is a line in between)
>
> reverse—to show what already happened or to be funny ("It really isn't happening backwards; it's just the TV pictures.")
>
> voice-over—to tell us something that we can't see in the picture ("You can't see the person, but he or she is in the TV studio, talking, but not to the camera.")
>
> animation—to show characters or to do things differently than regular people ("The TV artists make many, many different pictures of the character; then the camera person takes a picture of them all in a row, going really quickly.")

3 ✳ MAGAZINE TRICKS, OR BIG PICTURES LOOK FANCY

The tricks used in magazine graphics are similar to those in books, but with the addition of the visual conventions of advertisements. It's never too early to explain to your child that ads exaggerate. You can do this by saying that ads have ways of making us want to buy the product, even though we may not need it or even want it.

Magazine methods   Page through a glossy consumer magazine with your child, asking him or her to stop and point at whatever seems interesting. Then ask _why_ that thing seems interesting. (More magazine advertising is found in Chapter Eleven: The Basic Community.) Work in the following ideas:

> big pictures usually get our attention better than little pictures
>
> color pictures usually get our attention better than black and white pictures
>
> an unusual picture gets our attention (a person riding a giraffe, a fried egg on an air conditioner and so on)
>
> old-fashioned or confusing pictures get our attention because they're unusual
>
> the style of letters used in the ad makes us feel a certain way (big bold-faced ones look as though they're shouting; scrolly-looking ones often look fancy, thin ones sometimes remind us of thinness and so on)
>
> an interesting-looking face gets our attention

Point out that all these magazine tricks work well on billboards, too.

Faces   Have your child page through another magazine with you, looking only for interesting faces. Each time he or she finds one, ask how that person feels—sad, happy, excited, exuberant or any new word that seems appropriate. (More games on facial expressions are found in Chapter Three: Basic Concepts and Chapter Twenty: Body Language.)

Find that ad Page through a different magazine with your child, asking him or her to find ads. (This can be done before or after the child can read.)

Ask your child, "What do you think they want us to buy? How do they make it look? Would they show those clothes on an ugly person?" Teach a healthy skepticism!

4 ✳ PUNCTUATION GAMES, OR WHAT GOES POP?

To teach a beginning awareness of punctuation marks, read your child a familiar story, adding a different sound for each type of punctuation mark you encounter. Point to it at the same time. (This is an old comedy routine that *Electric Company* has adapted.) Make up your own sounds, with your child's help. A period could be "pop," an exclamation point a "wow" or a "yeeooww-pop" and so on. Explain that we need punctuation marks to tell us where to pause as we read, the expression to use when ending sentences and so on. (More advanced punctuation games are found in Chapter Fifteen: Reading.)

5 ✳ MAPS AND GLOBES, OR NORTH IS UP

These games introduce your child to some of the visual techniques used on maps and globes. Make sure to tell the child that they are merely the artist's methods and that the equator isn't really a ridge or a line—you could cross it in a boat and never know you had done so.

Strange lines Get out one or more maps and a globe and show your child the following:

The North Pole and the South Pole. No
"pole" is actually there, and you
wouldn't be on the top of any hill if you
were standing in either place.

North, South, East and West. On a flat map,
North is up, South is down, East is right
and West is left. After emphasizing this,
guide the child's finger around the world
to show that East really becomes West.
And try to convey the idea that a little
east from your city is different than a
little east from another city.

The equator. On a globe, it is around the
fattest part, the tummy, of the world. It is
always hot there. (It's not a real line, but
map and globe makers mark it that way
so we know where it is.)

Boundaries of states and countries. They are
drawn as lines but you will never find
them on an actual road. People need to
know different boundaries in order to
understand which laws they must obey.

Remember to explain that everything on a map or
globe is made much smaller than it really is. Otherwise,
we couldn't see countries, states or cities all at once and
the globe would have to be as big as the world. This is
why streets sometimes appear as lines and lakes as
puddles.

6 ✳ SYMBOLS, OR A HEART MEANS LOVE

The games here are easy in one sense and hard in
another. Your child may learn what stands for what (and
gain some cultural understanding), but may not under-

stand the meaning of symbols in everyday life. It is, however, a good start.

Basic symbols   With book and magazine pictures, or with your own drawings, teach your child that the following pictures are "symbols," shortcut ways of reminding us of longer things:

heart (love)   snowflake (winter)
star (a prize)   colored leaf (fall)
flower (springtime or   flag (a specific
    youth)   country)

More symbols   As above, but with:

hot sun (summer or warmth)
ethnic clothing (for a specific group, as in
    lederhosen for Germany)
Christmas tree (Christmas, giving)
turkey dinner (Thanksgiving or Christmas)
cross (Jesus)
menorah (Jewish candelabrum)

Your own special cultural symbols   As above.

7 ✳ WHAT OUR EYES CAN'T SEE AT ALL, OR FLIES HAVE HAIRY EYES

Beyond the boundary of normal vision are those things which only a special camera can see. These are not really visual conventions, but they are so eye-opening to the child that it is worth a trip to the library to get an adult book of electron-micrograph pictures or stop-action photographs.

Weird things   Show your child that flies have little hairs coming out of their eyes (if we look really closely) and that a milk drop forms a crown when it splashes on a counter and so on, whatever the book features. These everyday wonders will excite your child and may also remind him or her to look at the world in new ways.

Chapter Nine: Music

The learning games in this section are designed to help your child learn a little bit about musical concepts. They introduce such areas as basic notes, basic rhythm, music punctuation, musical instruments, musical moods, variety of music and song identification.

The enjoyment of music, and of learning about it, is a good preparation for leisure-time activities in childhood and adulthood. (And one of the surest cures for two grouchy children is one Strauss waltz and four hugs.) The sheer joy of making music is an expressive outlet that everyone should have a chance to develop. These games provide a simple beginning. Please do not, however, consider them a substitute for playing a wide variety of children's songs, folk tunes, jazz, rock, opera and various kinds of classical and other music for your children at other times, or for listening to live open-air concerts, participating in sing-alongs, or even for buying your child a little record player for a birthday or Christmas present. (For other music games, see Chapter Twenty-Three: Make Up a Song.)

Babies, toddlers and preschoolers can all enjoy and learn from these games, though they are too complicated for babies to actually master.

1 ✳ BASIC NOTES, OR SING HIGH AND LOW

Here your child can learn that music consists of pleasant or interesting sounds arranged in some sort of order. Take turns imitating each other as you make some music in the following ways.

Sing high and low   Sing a few individual high notes and ask your child to imitate you. Sing, "These are high notes." Do the same with a few medium-range and very low notes.

Then ask your child to sing a high note for *you* to imitate, then a medium one and then a low one.

Sing loud and soft   Sing a simple song (such as "Twinkle, Twinkle, Little Star") very softly and then very loudly. Tell your child that music sung softly is "pianissimo" and music sung loudly is "fortissimo." Have the child do both.

Tap high and low   Fill several glasses to different levels with water. Show your child how to tap the side of each one of them with a fork. Then have him or her "play" each of "our new musical instruments."

Decide together which are, generally speaking, high, medium and low notes and arrange them in a row from low to high (left to right).

Then ask your child to make up a little song by tapping the glasses.

The scale   Teach your child how to sing "do-re-mi-fa-sol-la-ti-do." Point out that our voices are also musical instruments and that each of these "scales" can also be called an "octave." Then teach the child to sing the scale backwards, too.

A tune   Sing a few simple tunes for your child (a *Sesame Street* song, for example), telling him or her that these are "tunes." Then ask your child to sing you a simple tune.

2 ✳ BASIC RHYTHM, OR TAP ALONG

These games will show your child that most music has rhythm or "a beat." Besides teaching a little music, they are also good practice in listening and paying attention.

Pots and pans   Collect several pots and pans of different sizes and materials and turn them over, drum-style. (Two is enough for a toddler, more for older children.) Also assemble two long-handled kitchen spoons.

Then ask your child to listen carefully. You tap out a simple three- or four-beat "da-da-dum-da." Now your child is to repeat it. Then lengthen the musical phrase to the limits your child can handle.

Next the child taps out a "drum song" and you repeat it. Finish with a clattering, free-for-all chorus!

In time   Find or sing a song with a simple beat, such as "Row, Row, Row Your Boat" or "Twinkle, Twinkle, Little Star." Show your child how to clap in time to the music, then tap a foot in time to it. Then, if your child is old enough, he or she should sing a song so you can keep time.

3 ✳ MUSIC PUNCTUATION, OR STACCATO IS POPCORN POPPING

"Musical punctuation" of various types can be illustrated with everyday objects. This will turn sounds into a kind of smorgasbord of activities.

Do it   Tell your child about the following kinds of musical punctuation. Have him or her act them out and, if possible, think of another example for each.

> staccato—snappy, short notes that sound like popping popcorn, snapping fingers or snapping elastic (then sing any song this way)
>
> legato—gliding, longer notes that seem like sliding along on ice skates or on a linoleum floor in socks (then sing any song this way)

Do the tempos   Similar to "musical punctuation," these are four new words for the tempo or the speed of music.

> prestissimo—as fast as possible, like clapping very fast (now sing any song this way)
>
> allegro—gay and cheerful like skipping (then sing any song this way)
>
> adagio—medium-slow and easygoing like sauntering along (then sing any song this way)
>
> largo—very slow, like a turtle in a parade (then sing any song this way)

Sounds that go and sounds that don't   Teach your child harmony (sounds right) and dissonance (sounds "off" but interesting) by creating a chord with a note your child sings. Do this by asking the child to sing any note—and hold it—while you sing another. If the notes sound as though they are fighting, that is dissonance.

4 ✳ MUSICAL INSTRUMENTS, OR TOOT LIKE A TUBA

These games introduce your child to musical instruments, each with its different voice.

To begin   Use any toy instruments you may have around at home—drums, horns, etc.—teaching the name and sound of each.

Record introductions   Check out a record from the library which introduces the musical instruments and their sounds to children. The following are some suggestions:

Peter and the Wolf   *Young Person's*
Tubby the Tuba   *Guide to the*
Sparky's Piano   *Orchestra*

Shopping to music   Here Mini-School can be combined with a shopping trip. Explore a nearby musical instruments store and get a little discreet hands-on experience and identification of several new instruments.

Toot   Teach your child to make the sounds of some of the musical instruments:

toot like a tuba   boom like a drum
toooot-tooot like a   eeek-eek like a
     trombone   piccolo

crash like cymbals   thrum, thrum like a
                                     bass violin
. . . and whatever else you can physically do

Instrument families   Teach your child that string instruments, percussion instruments and woodwinds are
the three main instrument families. Use a picture or a trip
to a music store to show string instruments like the violin
and cello; percussion instruments like the xylophone,
drum and chimes; and woodwind instruments like the
flute, clarinet and oboe.

Extra   If you have access to a piano or other instrument, teach your child how to play a scale and a few
chords, both harmonic and dissonant. Also teach a few
basic parts of the instrument.

5 ✳ MUSICAL MOODS, OR THAT SOUNDS GLOOMY

These games will teach your child to become sensitive
to music and to listen carefully. They may even help him
or her learn to alter a mood by listening to music (surely
better than doing it chemically).

Sad or glad?   Play or sing for your child two or three
short selections that vary considerably in their mood. Ask
the child how each one makes him or her feel. If it
applies, explain, generally, the idea of major and minor
keys (the latter usually, but not always, sound a bit sad).

Bees buzzing?   Find, in the library or at home, some
representational music—perhaps notes that sound like
bees buzzing, or wind blowing. Play it for your child and

ask what it sounds like. Remember to stress that most music isn't this way.

Art and music   Play two short selections of music that differ considerably in mood, asking your child to listen to them. At the same time, have him or her draw a picture while the first selection plays, then another as the second selection plays.

If the pictures differ in any significant way, ask your child why one is, for example, a monster and the other an ocean. Was it because the Dvořák and the Debussy music were so different in mood? Does music affect our moods? (If both pictures were trucks or tulips, forget "the message"!)

6 ✳ PLAY MUSIC, OR ROCK IS NOT OPERA

To make sure that your child knows how many different kinds of music there are, introduce many of them.

Play it   Play for your child a record player potpourri, a minute's worth of five wildly different types of music—rock, opera, folk, baroque, classical or new wave music, for example. Tell your child the names, and then ask which were his or her favorites.

7 ✳ NAME THAT TUNE, OR THAT'S TWINKLE, TWINKLE

To help your child put together the beginning of a musical memory and to build his or her listening skills, try the old "Name That Tune" game.

Name it   Hum a familiar song (without the words) and

ask your child to tell you the name of it. Then sing another and have the child tell you the name of this one as soon as he or she knows what it is, preferably after only a few musical phrases or even notes. Next, the child hums and you guess.

If your child is quite musical, he or she may be able to identify songs as you tap their rhythm on the table or from the few bars before the lyrics begin on records. Mine never could, but some children can even begin to identify classical music this way.

Chapter Ten: Science Tricks

WHAT, WHY AND WHO

The learning games in this section are designed to intrigue your child with science—what happens and why. They will help your child learn observing and recording, measuring, how materials change, how to form theories, abstract processes and scientific equipment.

The games should encourage the natural curiosity of your child, who has probably already asked stump-the-parent questions like, "Why is the sky blue?" and, "Where did the first monkey come from?" In some ways, scientists are merely grown-up children who have never stopped asking questions like these.

Please don't worry if you don't know all the answers. No one does. The point is to be interested in scientific happenings and to learn how to look for them. Tell your child that, in many cases, scientists are still studying these things; even they don't know all the answers to many of our "why" questions.

While playing these games, reinforce your child's interest in adult science, too, by calling him or her a "kid chemist" or a "kid ecologist" as you do games relating to these areas. And make sure to introduce the new science vocabulary words as you go along. All this should make your child more eager to take science courses later.

Your child *will* be a scientist here because most of the games involve learning by doing. In a few cases (such as measuring) they may require motor skills too advanced for your child. If so, help. The idea here is to develop your child's conceptual skills. The games teach careful thinking skills—how to approach a question or problem, for example. And many games reinforce number skills, as well as reading and writing.

Most of these games are too complicated for babies or even toddlers. (For preliminary versions of some of them, see Chapter Four: Basic Knowledge.) They are best suited for preschoolers. (For an extension of some of the fact-seeking methods, see Chapter Fourteen: Fun Facts and How to Find Them.)

Remember that the activities and game groups themselves proceed (roughly) from easier to harder. Find five minutes of activities for each Mini-School session. (Some games here can be set up as part of one session, then finished on subsequent days.)

1 ✳ OBSERVING AND RECORDING, OR HOW A KID SCIENTIST STARTS

The games here can begin in your kitchen or yard. Not only is there much to learn nearby (what ants eat, for example, or how squirrels find their buried nuts), but the basics of observing, recording and classifying can be demonstrated most easily in these accessible areas.

Mixing   Assemble some food coloring vials and fill several glasses half-full of water. Let your "kid chemist" experiment with what happens when he or she mixes yellow and blue, red and yellow, blue and yellow. After these key combinations, proceed up to the muddiest purple-brown imaginable!

Explain to your child that red, yellow and blue are called the "primary colors." This means that all the other colors can be mixed from them.

Collecting I   Have your "kid ecologist" collect a set of four to eight different tree leaves. Then classify them in some way, perhaps from the darkest green to the lightest green, from the biggest to the smallest, or according to their place of origin (evergreen or deciduous trees), for example.

Then your child should tape or paste them onto a piece of paper or cardboard titled something like "Scientist's Report: Neighborhood Leaves." (Make sure the child does at least part of the writing.)

Collecting II   As above, but with rocks or shells.

Collecting III   As above, but with bugs or weeds.

Collecting IV   As above, but with flowers or sticks.

Watching Animals   Discovering the habits of ordinary living things can be a lot of fun for parents as well as for children. Start with ants, squirrels, robins, sparrows, pigeons or neighborhood dogs and cats. Observe any animal's movements and territory, its eating preferences, its way of protecting itself or its daily schedule.

To discover what ants like to eat and when, for example, locate an anthill that is likely to remain undisturbed by cars or people for twenty-four hours. Then ask your child to choose four or five kitchen foods as "ant choices." (Make sure one of the foods is high in natural sugar, such as a bit of fruit, and another is greasy, such as a smudge of margarine.) Then ask your child how we should set out the food so that the ants have a chance to show us which food they really like best. Depending on your child's age and savvy, he or she may not figure out that the food choices should be equidistant from, or in a circle around, the anthill. If not, suggest it. Then have your child set out the food.

To discover the food preference, make sure to check early in the morning or in the evening that day or the next day (these are their most common mealtimes). Do you see any ants wolfing anything down? What looks chewed on?

Classifying I   This next game goes beyond the collecting games above to teach your child a more abstract method of classifying or grouping. Explain to your child that the way to classify all the things around us is by grouping them in the three main categories of animal, vegetable and mineral. Use several examples from each group to illustrate the differences—such as dog, bird and person for animal, tomato and banana for vegetable, and rock, sand and metal for mineral. Then ask your child for additional examples.

Next have him or her lead you on a scavenger hunt around the house or yard and find two or more examples of each category.

Classifying II   Tell your child that the "animal" category can be divided into even more groups because we like animals so much and want to know about so many of them.

The categories to explain here are mammal, bird, insect, reptile and fish—and remember to use plenty of examples. Then page through a child's word book, picture dictionary or related book with your child, asking him or her to match the animal with the appropriate category. Work in a few "fun facts" and some flexibility by explaining, for example, that the first bird on earth didn't look like the one in the picture. It was just beginning to get feathers and could fly only a little bit.

2 ✳ MEASURING, OR HOW LONG IS YOUR FOOT?

The games here help your child to measure things, one method used by scientists to learn more about the world. Begin with things close to your child's experience, but tell him or her that we *could* measure almost anything—from the height of houses (architects do) to the number of leaves consumed by little bugs (zoologists do).

Measure me—length   Use a ruler, yardstick or measuring tape to show your child how to measure length, or how long something is. Teach the words "inch" or "centimeter" and "foot," and show how to start with the "one" and how to find the numbers on the measuring device.

Then place your child's hands and feet on a piece of paper. Have your child help you measure their length. The result might make a nice gift. (Don't measure the width of the foot at this time and don't discuss fractions. Merely say them yourself, "two and one-half inches long" or whatever.)

Measure me—height   With your child's heels against a wall, you can easily measure his or her height, or tallness, in feet and inches. (Save this measurement so you can compare it with his or her height later.) At this point, mention the basic fractions—one quarter, one half and three quarters—so that your child becomes accustomed to hearing the words.

Measure me—width   Choose a simple object, such as a box, and show your child the width—how wide something is.

Then measure the length *and* height *and* width of a simple favorite toy such as a small doll.

Measure me—weight   Tell your child that another kind of measurement is weight, or how heavy something is. Begin by weighing him or her on a typical bathroom scale. Show your child how to read the result and record it on a chart.

Then, if you own a small kitchen scale, you and your child can weigh various foods. Ask him or her to choose any two food items—perhaps a jar of honey and a tomato. Then the child should hold one item in each hand and guess which is heavier. Check the answer by weighing the items. Have your child read off the main number and add the fraction or the ounces yourself.

Explain at this point that one quarter is *one* part if the pound is divided into *four* parts; one half is *one* part if it is divided into *two* parts; and three quarters is *three* parts if it is divided into *four* parts. Take some easily divided object, such as a piece of cheese, and cut it into two, then four, parts to barely demonstrate this quite difficult idea.

Measure me—volume I   The only difficult aspect of this game is the word "volume," another kind of measurement. Tell your child that it means "how much there is of something pourable."

Take out a measuring cup and a quart or gallon jar if you have them. Ask your child what pourable thing he or she would like to measure. (Milk, water, flour, chocolate chips and so on.) Again, stress one quarter, one half and three quarters by pointing out the lines on the measuring cup and having your child help you read them.

Measure me—volume II   Play another measuring game, this one using a tablespoon, teaspoon and half teaspoon. Let your child see that two half teaspoons of salt equal one teaspoon. Make sure the child does all or most of the pouring. Then play around with measuring other items of your child's choice with these units.

Measuring free-for-all   Grab a ruler, measuring cup and the scales and have your child lead you around the house, apartment or yard measuring the length, height, width, depth, weight and/or volume of anything your child chooses.

3 ✳ CHANGES IN MATERIALS, OR IT'S GETTING SQUISHY

Just as a child keeps growing, things in our world keep changing, too. Some change rapidly, like margarine softening when it is removed from the refrigerator; others change *very* slowly, like rocks turning into sand. (Early versions of some of these games are found in Chapter Four: Basic Knowledge.)

Fast changes I   Have your child observe a fast change such as margarine softening. Remove one stick of margarine from the refrigerator or freezer. Then prepare a "Scientist's Report," beginning with something like "7:30 a.m.—margarine very hard." Then have your child touch the margarine and record something like "7:35 a.m.—margarine softer."

Fast changes II   As above, but this time use an egg. First shake the egg, then drop it into some boiling water until it hardens. (You may want to crack open another egg before the boiling process, just as a means for comparison.) Then shake the hard-boiled egg and cut it open. Record the results.

Fast changes III   As above, but now you can demonstrate how very hot water cools. Begin with water as hot as is safe. If you own a thermometer, begin with some very hot water in a pan and record its temperature. Wait a few minutes until it cools, then measure the temperature once more. If you do not own a thermometer, simply use hot water that is safe to touch. To measure the change, use words such as "very hot" and "cool."

Other changes, in liquid   Boil a small amount of water in a tea kettle. When the steam starts to emerge, have your child feel it, at a safe distance. Then hold a cup around the spout. Presto—the steam condenses on the inside of the cup and turns back into water.

Then keep the heat on so your child can see how all the water converts into steam. Explain to your child that condensation on a car windshield or window, steam over a warm lake on a cool morning, fog and clouds are very similar to steam. They are all water vapor.

Slower changes   Here your child can see a slower change—how things spoil when they get old, for example. You will particularly examine which foods rot and which dry out. (An earlier version of this game is in Chapter Four: Basic Knowledge.) Ask your child to choose four or five bits of food. (Perhaps leftover food that you were going to discard or bits of outdoor plants.) Set them on an indoor counter.

Ask your child which foods might rot and which might dry out. Prepare the "Scientist's Report" with the names of the food, date and columns for "dried out" and "rotted."

Then, when the results are clear, complete the report in Mini-School. (If you have grapes and a hot, sunny day, you might also try drying grapes to make raisins. Put them on aluminum foil away from the birds and turn them several times during the day.)

Even slower changes I   Monitor slower changes like those listed below. Begin by preparing your "Scientist's Report," listing the name of the process, the date begun and the concluding date. Then show your child how to mark a later date on a family calendar, when the process should be checked again for changes (perhaps in a week or a month, in another Mini-School). Start with one of the following:

> Fingernails growing. Begin on a day your child's nails should be clipped. Remember to record the date when they need to be clipped again.
>
> Hair growing. Begin when your child's hair is fairly long and measure its length from the crown forward. Then, after the next haircut, record its length again.

Even slower changes II   As above, but choose one of the following:

> Mud washing away. Set out a clump of mud where you can see it. Watch it change as rain washes over it and it "erodes."
>
> Sandstone into sand. If you can find any sandstone or other soft stone, help your child grind it into sand. Then explain that with hard rocks, this process takes many,

many years to complete. In fact, once all
our beach sand was rocks.

Animal changes   Depending on the local wildlife, you
and your child can observe and record animal changes
like the following. Begin in one Mini-School and finish
approximately one month later.

the hair length of an outdoor dog

the fatness of squirrels

the awakening or bedtime of birds

the turning of a caterpillar into a butterfly. (If
you can catch a black woolly caterpillar in
late summer, put it into a jar with leaves
on the bottom and holes in the lid. Keep
feeding it fresh leaves until the weather
gets cold. Then stop feeding it, but keep
its "home" outside. When it wakes up in
the spring start feeding it again. Then it
may treat you to a cocoon and rebirth
once the weather is reliably warm.)

4 ✳ MAKING THEORIES, OR SCIENTISTS THINK HARD

The games in this group will help your child think of
explanations for a few key phenomena in the animal and
vegetable worlds. They are not as complex as you might
imagine, at least not for an older preschooler. Remind
your child that scientists are always looking for answers
to "why" questions.

Pretend   Ask your child to pretend to be a little seed
on a dandelion or other familiar plant. How will you get
planted so that you can grow into a new plant?

Accept all answers, just telling your child in some cases, "Well, dandelions don't do it that way, but burr plants surely do," and so on. Your child's theories and your extra explanations should include ones like these—a person will plant me; I will blow in the wind and then the rain will push me down into the dirt; I will stick on the fur of an animal and then get brushed off somewhere else; I will get buried into the ground by a squirrel or other animal and then forgotten. Next act out some of these theories with your child.

Two questions   Ask your child to think of one answer to fit both of these questions—why does a turtle need a shell *and* why does a tiny baby bird need to grow inside an egg?

Then explain the idea of "protection," or staying safe. Ask your child to think of ways in which other animals protect themselves. Your "kid biologist" may come up with some answers like these—birds protect themselves by flying away, squirrels by scrambling up trees, cats by clawing and by climbing up trees, people by living in houses (or, in the old, old days, in caves).

Hard to see   Ask your child why it is difficult to see bugs crawling on the bark of a tree *and* to see sparrows on the dirt. Then introduce the idea of "camouflage," another form of protection. Ask your child to think of other examples—a robin in a bush, a frog in a pond, a fish in the water, etc.

Next explain that not all animals use camouflage. Elephants, for example, are so large and strong that camouflage is not necessary. Others have bright colors so that they can show off and find a mate—a cardinal bird in a tree does not want to be hidden and has another good protection anyway (it can fly away).

Finding what they need   Ask your child why a bear might have claws while a deer does not. Then explain that each kind of animal has certain body parts as a means of finding food. The bear uses its claws to grab a fish out of a river or a small animal out of a hiding place. The deer needs to paw at the ground to get grass even when there is snow on the ground in winter, and it also needs the hoofs to run well.

Then ask your child why a whale needs to be able to hold its breath for a long time. And why an eagle has "talons" on its feet.

Sharing I   Ask your child why some animals stay up all night and sleep all day while other animals do the opposite. Then explain that the former are called "nocturnal animals" (owls and, usually, raccoons, for example). The night is their "share of the world," their "ecological niche." They take the night shift, so that all the animals aren't bumping into each other all the time, trying to get food. Name, if you can, more nocturnal animals.

Sharing II   Tell your child that not all shares of the world or "ecological niches" are for day or nighttime eating. Animals also share *places* in the world. Ask him or her where a bird's place is. (Mostly up in the air and in trees or bushes.) This "niche" is good protection for the bird, too.

Then ask your child what share of the world or "ecological niche" squirrels have? How about honey bees?

5 ✳   MORE PROCESSES, OR WHAT ELSE IS REALLY
GOING ON AROUND HERE?

The games here draw your child's attention to some of
the more abstract and mysteriously intriguing processes
in the world. Through them, he or she can also learn
some new words. (Earlier games on natural processes are
found in Chapter Four: Basic Knowledge and in game
groups 1 and 3 of this section.)

Gravity   Give your child two unbreakable objects and
ask him or her to drop them. Then, without saying a
word, ask your child to jump as high as possible. Next
ask, "What happens to everything or everybody that goes
up?" Tell your child that the name for this downward
pushing force is "gravity." It pulls everything toward the
center of the earth. Ask him or her to think of other
things that go down (rain, spilt milk, rocks rolling down
hills and so on).

Next, illustrate the way gravity works on the moon.
Explain that the moon is smaller than our earth, so its
gravity isn't as strong as ours. The moon's gravity pulls
everything down toward the center of the moon, but not
as strongly. Lift your child into leaping, floating jumps,
telling him or her that astronauts moved like this on the
moon, because gravity is weaker there.

Molecules move around   Choose a fragrant flower or
food, one that your child can smell from a couple of steps
away (choose, for example, a bouquet of marigolds or
minced onion spice). Ask your child to sniff and smell it.

Then explain that a smell is made up of tiny particles
called molecules which hop off things and get into the air
near our noses. Add that everything in the world is made
up of these tiny molecules.

Next, let your child tear a flower petal, then smell something being heated up—like chocolate melting or a hamburger cooking. Ask if these smells are strong too. Then add that tearing or heating makes more molecules jump off into the air. (You may want to point out to sensitive children that molecules in the air aren't like bugs nor will they do anything bad to our noses.)

Evaporation   Have your child fill a measuring cup with water exactly to the halfway point and explain that the scientists are going to study "evaporation" today. This is the way molecules of water or other liquid jump up into the air, very gradually. It's a much slower process than something cooking. (A simpler version of this game is found in Chapter Four: Basic Knowledge.)

Set out the water where no one will drink it. And prepare, with your child, the "Scientist's Report" format, including the amount of water, today's date and title, "Evaporation."

After that, check the water every two or three days in Mini-School and record the date when it hits one third of a cup, one quarter of a cup and zero. Tell your child that on days when there's a lot of water already in the air ("humid days"), less of our water will evaporate.

Displacement   Fill another measuring cup halfway with water. Then ask your child to drop small sinkable objects, like pebbles, into the liquid. What happens to the water? Why?

Explain that the water and the pebbles can't both be in the same place at the same time. So the water has to move up to get out of the way.

(If you can, demonstrate this at bath time too. Before your child gets in, mark the water level with a small smear of soap on the side of the tub. Then see how high the water rises to get out of the way of your child.)

Friction   Ask your child to rub his or her hands together very forcefully and quickly. Do they feel different now? Next have the child rub a smooth toy on a smooth table in the same manner. How does it feel different?

Then explain that this is "friction." Rubbing two objects together in an energetic fashion makes their molecules jiggle a lot, and so they get warmer.

If you're especially energetic and have time on a dry day, try rubbing two sticks together to make a fire like "the cave people" did. (This takes a long time.)

6 ✻ SCIENTIFIC GIZMOS

These games will intrigue your child with scientific apparatus. Only very basic explanations are necessary. Just have your child play "kid scientist" and learn a few new words and tricks in the process.

The basics   Let your child experiment with the following gizmos:

> A magnet. Have a treasure hunt for "ferrous metals." Then tell your child that a magnet works when the little bits of one object are attracted to the little bits of the other object.
> A sieve. Have your child pour various smooth and lumpy substances through it to see what happens. Or make a little bit of freshly squeezed orange juice—even with

one orange—to show how a sieve lets the juice through but not the pulp.

More   As above, but with:

A funnel. It makes pouring easier, especially from a large container to a smaller one.

A magnifying glass. Go on another exploration, this time looking at things close up. And don't forget parts of the body like taste buds and hair. Explain that the special glass makes everything look bigger than it actually is.

Still more   As above, but with:

A teeter-totter. Really one kind of "fulcrum," it balances weights and makes heavy things—like a big, big kid—easier to lift. Experiment with small objects of different weights on a prebalanced teeter-totter, too.

Sandpaper. Friction from sandpaper scraping on wood not only heats up the wood, but it also wears it away. Try sanding other objects, too.

Exotics   Look around for more unusual scientific equipment you might have on hand:

A prism. In a prismlike vase or a real rainbow, the sunlight is split into all its hidden colors.

A gyroscope. The spinning keeps the whole thing balanced.

Or any one of many possible birthday or Christmas presents under $10 (e.g., a snowflake preservation kit or soil testing kit).

Chapter Eleven: The Basic Community

The learning games in this section are designed to teach your child a little bit about living in a community and about how communities of people began. The games demonstrate the basics of where food comes from and how it is preserved; how our clothes and our homes are constructed; what main geographical features are in our world and our community; what newspapers and magazines tell us about our community; how money works; how laws work and a little bit about our ancestors.

To many modern city children, flour comes from a grocery store, houses and clothes always existed in their present form and money is paper we get at the bank. Because children don't initially comprehend the basics of community life, they cannot fully appreciate what we have. In these games, understanding is created partly by providing the perspective of earlier cultures (what "the cave kid" did) and partly by learning-by-doing games. Both should intrigue your child and encourage him or her to remain curious about the ways of cultures. This is also a good area in which to consider a commuters' Mini-School or a weekend field trip, with time to get out and look at a construction site, the freight entrance of a grocery store or a bank's safety deposit boxes.

155

These games are all for preschoolers. Choose one of those below for your five-minute session.

1 ✱ FOOD, OR WHAT DID PEOPLE DO BEFORE THERE WERE GROCERY STORES?

Once upon a time there were no grocery stores. The purpose of this group of learning games is to help your child discover how people used to find food. Begin by asking your child what he or she would eat for lunch if we had no refrigerator or cupboards filled with a vast array of foods—and no grocery stores.

Then follow with one of the following activities—and a strong warning about poisonous plants.

Growing food   Have your child plant several tomato or zucchini seeds in paper cups. Make sure the seeds are well covered with dirt. Explain that "kid farmers" plant several seeds because not every seed sprouts the way it is supposed to. Then care for the sprouts together, watering and repotting as necessary.

Making basic food   Choose one of the following foods to make "from scratch" like people did in the "old days."

> squeeze oranges into orange juice
> squish blueberries into blueberry juice
> make nut butter with nuts and a little oil
> shake cream in a tightly closed glass jar until
>   you get butter (this will take 45 minutes
>   to an hour).

Making flour for bread   Although this is difficult, even a small result can be tasted and the effect appreciated.

You will need a slightly larger than hand-sized blunt rock for each of you and a medium-sized cardboard box (unless, of course, you have a real mortar-and-pestle–shaped rock or wood combination). Take turns pounding raw rice, popcorn or other grain in the box until some of it gets powdery. That's your flour! If you plan to make bread or cookies any time soon, add some of it to your regular store-bought flour.

Preserving food   Ask your child what happens to food we leave sitting around too long. (It either dries out or rots). Then "show and tell" some of the ways people preserved food before refrigerators were invented:

> put it with ice (cubes) in a cool place or even
> underground
> added lots of salt to it
> added lots of sugar to it (fruits made into jam)
> dried it in the sun or near a fire

Plant a garden I   If you have time for this project, begin a series of weekend Mini-Schools on gardening. For the first one, make a list of what you will plant, with your child doing all or most of the writing.

Plant a garden II   Choose the seeds from a catalog or seed rack. Make sure your child helps with the reading.

Plant a garden III   Hoe the soil.

Plant a garden IV   Plant the seeds, with your child helping to label the rows.

Plant a garden V   Weed your garden. As you do so,

teach your child the idea of weeds crowding our plants and explain the main parts of a plant (root, leaf, seed and so on).

Plant a garden VI   Harvest and process your produce together.

2 ✳ SHELTER, OR WHERE DO CLOTHES AND HOUSES COME FROM?

With these activities, your child can learn a little bit about how people used to make clothes and living places.

Cloth   Assemble a handful of very long dried grasses or six-inch-long strings or ribbons. Set the pieces out in a gridwork pattern so both of you can weave them together, under and over, to get a small piece of "cloth." (It could become a hat, a doll's cloak or a child's "tummy-warmer.")

Then show your child pieces of cotton and other commercial cloth close up, to see how machines now weave for us.

Colored cloth   Choose an old rag or undershirt, or even a nice white T-shirt, if you prefer, to dye into colored cloth. Boil it with something like marigold flowers, blueberries, onion skins, beet juice or loose tea leaves, all of which should work reasonably well.

Then also experiment with whatever nearby natural plants or foods your child chooses as dyes, including some that you suspect won't work (because they wash right out). Explain to your child that "cave people" had to try lots of plants because the colors of many of them wash out easily in water. (Make sure your child is not frightened by a confusion of "dye" with "die"!)

Cave person clothes   Have your child find some large leaves that the two of you can sew together for a temporary vest.

Primitive pillows   Ask your child what we could stuff inside a small rag pouch to make a soft pillow if we couldn't buy one at the store. Proceed to actually stuff the pouch.

Simple shelter I   On a rainy day, find a very large leaf and a fairly long stick. Have your child poke the stick an inch or so through the center of the leaf. Held over the head, this is a basic umbrella. Another suggestion is to use a tree branch, with its own leaves serving as part of the "umbrella."

Simple shelter II   On a dry day, take your child outside and ask how a cave girl or cave boy would sweep the walk or the rocks in the front of the cave. Then do it.

Not-so-simple shelter   If you are really ambitious some weekend, get three long sticks (at least four feet long) and an old sheet to make a teepee.
   Poke three sticks into the ground so that their tops lean together and their other ends splay out several feet apart. Tie the tops together. Drape an old sheet around them. Presto—a teepee!

3 ✳ FEATURES OF OUR WORLD, OR THE WILDEST GEOGRAPHY TRIPS EVER

   This set of learning games teaches your child a basic understanding of volcanoes, oceans, rivers, meadows, jungles, forests, mountains and the North and South poles. The child acts out these geography "lessons."

Volcanoes   Explain that volcanoes "erupt" or explode with lava, steam and ashes. Set the scene by saying, "You're the volcano Mt. St. Helens in Washington or Mauna Loa in Hawaii. Geologists are studying you and measuring you and think you'll erupt any minute."

Then you both crouch down and erupt, "cheke-ewww."

Oceans   Add salt to water in a large container. Decide which ocean it should be, consulting a globe if possible. Then pretend to be the ocean, making waves against a beach in California or Africa or wherever. Taste it too.

Rivers   Pour water along a surface and watch where the river flows. Name it—perhaps the Mississippi or the Amazon—and tell your child where it flows. Illustrate on a globe, if possible.

Meadows   Describe the features of a meadow to your child. Then take turns being the birds, mice, chipmunks and so on that live there in the long grass.

Jungles   Describe and/or show pictures of a jungle to your child. Then pretend that both of you are hiking through the jungle in, for example, New Guinea or Brazil. What animals do you hear and see (the screech of a parrot, the chatter of a monkey)?

Forests   Act out forests in a similar fashion, catching sight of a deer, hearing a bird sing and so on.

Mountains   In the same make-believe fashion, climb high mountains until there are no more trees; here you are "past the timber line." Snow appears, then finally you reach the top and can see the valley below.

The South Pole and North Pole   Rub ice cubes on your cheeks, put on your imaginary coat and hike past polar bears (north), seals (both) and penguins (south).

Globe fun   With a globe, you can help your child find some of the above features. And he or she can become familiar with the names and locations of the continents and some of the countries. Emphasize the terms North and South and, just as in Chapter Eight: Visual Information, stress again that the equator is not really a ridge or a line. (My children also like to hear little tidbits about some of the countries, such as the fact that China is very crowded, Canada has two main languages, Mexico has new oil wells and so on, one mini-fact per country.)

4 ✳ NEIGHBORHOOD GEOGRAPHY, OR WHAT IS ALL AROUND HERE?

These games further acquaint your child with your neighborhood. This learning can progress from the backyard all the way to the nearest large shopping center, and from learning to list key features to making a real map. (Preliminary games for getting acquainted with the neighborhood are found in Chapter One: Basic Things, Chapter Four: Basic Knowledge and Chapter Seven: Daily Life.)

Yard map   Draw a very rough outline map for your child of your home and nearby yard or park boundaries. Ask him or her to tell you what's within the boundaries and where. Then your child can mark lines or make very simple drawings for these features on the map.

Neighborhood list   With your child, compile a list of the many buildings found in your neighborhood. Try to use broad definitions. Then, in list form, have the child help you group them by geographic area.

Neighborhood map   Next, help your child draw little squares for some of these neighborhood features on a basic map on which you've drawn the main streets. (This is easier if your child follows the outline of the main streets with a finger.)

Then help your child label some of the key features with abbreviations.

Street map   Using a street map of your community, help your child find key landmarks such as rivers, large highways, schools and so on. Ask him or her to find the "road path" or "route" we would use to drive from home to school.

Street trip   For a short trip sometime, take the bus together, following the map route with your fingers.

5 ✳ NEWSPAPERS, MAGAZINES AND THE TV NEWS, OR WHAT'S HAPPENING AND WHAT DO THEY WANT US TO BUY?

The games here introduce your child to the mass media and the many things we can learn from newspapers and magazines. Some of the games also promote a healthy awareness of sensationalized advertisements. (Games involving the news content of the paper and the newscast are found in Chapter Fourteen: Fun Facts and How To Find Them.)

Newspaper fun   Let your child page through your daily newspaper and ask questions about those things which touch his or her curiosity. In between these questions, teach your child to identify a headline, comic strip, picture spread, story and picture caption. Mention that the newspaper tells us what's happening throughout the world. Also explain why some stories have pictures and some don't. (For example, newspapers like to show pictures of famous people and of disasters.)

Likewise, point out advertisements and the reasons they are found in newspapers. (For example, stores and other companies pay to have their merchandise shown so that we'll see it and maybe buy it. Many times they make things sound better than they actually are—this is called exaggeration.)

Magazines   Give your child a consumer magazine and ask him or her to find you an ad. What is it advertising? Then point out something about the method of presentation—for example, if a company wants us to buy their perfume, would they show an ugly person wearing it? (Chapter Eight: Visual Information also includes a game on magazine graphics and how they work.)

Next, go through the whole magazine with your child, having him or her find other ads and read headlines, if possible.

Explain, too, what kinds of stories this particular magazine usually publishes.

TV news   Watch part of it with your child, explaining, mostly through responses to your child's questions, what's going on in the stories and ads.

6 ✳ How Money Works, or Sense About Dollars and Cents

These activities provide your child with a preview of the world of money—both counting and earning it. Even very small children can understand that adults work to earn money to purchase the things their families need and to save and invest some of it for the future. (More activities for understanding money are found in Chapter Twelve: Numbers and Chapter Fourteen: Fun Facts And How To Find Them.)

Counting money   Teach your child to identify the penny, nickel, dime, quarter, fifty-cent piece and $1 and $5 bills, and how much each is worth in pennies. You might give him or her some of the coins he or she can identify by the end of each session. Or let your child carry along some of the money needed to pay for groceries the next time you go shopping together. At home or at a store, also encourage your child to ask the cost of some of the items.

Earning money I   For a project that will take several Mini-School days and culminate in a long, weekend Mini-School, how about suggesting that your child set up a lemonade or granola stand?

The first step is to help your child list all the supplies needed—those to be bought (in one column) and those on hand (such as a card table, in the other).

Earning money II   The second step in this project includes three strategy decisions. First, decide with your child the quantity to sell in each container (the amount should equal a reasonable price). Then, compute what that will cost to produce (just mention your own arithmetic here). And last, decide what to charge so that you will earn a small, but reasonable, profit. Write it all down, with your child's help.

Earning money III   Choose your own location and make large signs.

Earning money IV   Do it! (When it is necessary to make change, just mention it to your child, but do it yourself.) Then count up your proceeds, dividing them into costs (the amount you paid for the supplies) and pure profit.

7 ✳ WHY LAWS STARTED, OR I'LL HIT YOU OVER THE HEAD

Ask your child what he or she thinks would happen if there were no laws (explained as "conduct rules for grown-ups") in the following areas.

Traffic laws, or car-driving   What would happen at "intersections"? And where might some adults park? What kind of rules do we need?

Assault, or hitting   What would happen if two big, strong adults got into a terrible fight? What kinds of laws would we want to have for hitting and hurting? Then explain, briefly, that we have many other kinds of laws, too. And add that we vote for senators and representatives, who then go to Washington, D.C., and to our state capital to make up new laws if we need them.

8 ✳ WHAT OUR ANCESTORS WERE LIKE, OR NO, WE CAN'T GO VISIT THEM

Each family possesses a personal sense of heritage stretching back as far as memories allow. Our heritage includes many ancestors originating from at least one foreign country. Even young children are not too young to appreciate their ancestors, though they will probably not understand why they can't go to visit them.

Family tree   Ask your child to help you draw a family tree, with you drawing the "branches" and the child adding the leaves at the end. Start with your child or children at the bottom and work up, leaving some blanks for your child to fill in with your help.

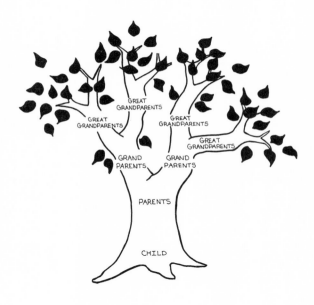

All Ancestors' Day   Teach your child the names of all his or her ancestors' countries and where to find them on a globe or map.

The reward for learning this could be a very special All Ancestors' Day Dinner, with one food from each of the countries (roast beef from Britain? Lefse from

Norway? German chocolate cupcakes from Germany?). Part of the dinner time can also be spent by telling stories about what it was like when Grandma was a little girl and how Great-Grandpa came over from Norway, and by answering the children's questions about their ancestors.

Chapter Twelve: Numbers

The learning games in this section are designed to introduce your child to the world of numbers. They begin with counting (building on skills from Chapter Three: Basic Concepts and Chapter Four: Basic Knowledge). They then present some practical uses of numbers, more advanced ways numbers are used, identifying and manipulating numbers and a sense of how numbers structure our world. (Consider them along with the other advanced learning games involving numbers in Chapter Ten: Science Tricks.)

These games build rote skills, an enjoyment of number play and a sense of the importance of numbers. But don't expect more than a basic understanding of number concepts and how numbers structure our thinking—the latter often doesn't come until late elementary school.

Building your child's confidence with numbers is a key goal of these games, too. This is especially important for girls. Schools still often project the subtle message that "math is for boys," an insidious idea that is worth trying to inoculate your child against (whether or not you are a mathematical genius yourself). Too much talent has been wasted and too many future job opportunities have been closed off for girls because of this idea.

168

Begin the early games even with a baby or toddler. Then proceed with your preschooler through the later, more difficult ones, choosing five minutes of activities for each Mini-School session.

1 ✳ MORE COUNTING, OR CLAP FIVE TIMES

Counting objects can be simple and enjoyable, though it is more complex than the sheer number memorizing of earlier Mini-School areas. It can even involve physical exercise.

Nearby things   With your child, count small groups of simple items such as trees in the yard, cracks in the sidewalk, stairs in the hall, chairs in the kitchen, etc. Have your child touch the items as you go along, since some children learn much better when the tactile sense is included.

Counting in rows and circles   Set out a *pile* of ten or fewer acorns, spools of thread or other small items. Ask your child to think of a way to count them so we won't get mixed up and count the same ones twice. The child may decide to arrange them in a long row, or pick them up one at a time or even place them in a circle.

Then teach him or her to count by touching each item, saying its number and *then* moving on to touch the next one (otherwise, we might say two numbers for one item by mistake).

Doing it   Ask your child to count aloud with you as he or she hops three times, then walks over and touches the refrigerator two times, then claps four times and so on with other counting actions.

Next, stretch your child's memory a little by asking

for two counting "jobs" at once—"clap three times, then touch the TV two times," for example. Proceed to three in a row. Also teach the words "once" and "twice."

Counting high   Review counting to 100 (in Chapter Four: Basic Knowledge). Then teach your child to count to 1,000 in a similar way—the "100 family" leads to the "200 family" and so on. (All this took my four-year-old almost four Mini-Schools, and I must say we won't do it again!)

2 ✱ WHAT NUMBERS ARE USED FOR, OR ONE CUP OF CHOCOLATE CHIPS NEXT

This set of activities shows your child the most elementary ways in which numbers are used (more are included in game groups 3 and 4 below). They will encourage your child to be aware of numbers and will demonstrate how important they are to our daily life.

Clocks   To show one place where numbers are important, unplug a clock, particularly one with very distinct numbers and lines. Ask your child to point and count "one o'clock, two o'clock" and so on as you move the hands around, hour by hour. Mention what your child would be doing at each hour.

Then explain that each day has twenty-four hours (which includes the daytime *and* the nighttime). And teach the words "clockwise" and "counterclockwise." Next, have your child review the numbers from one to twelve.

Telling time I   Start moving the hands around to demonstrate all the "o'clocks." For example, "the little hand is at the two and the big hand is at the twelve when it's two o'clock." Tell your child always to look at this little hand first, but to ignore the thin second hand, if there is one.

Telling time II   Next come all the thirties, the half-hours, along with a review of the o'clocks. ("The little hand is *after* the eight, so it's 8:30, thirty minutes after eight o'clock."

Telling time III   Next come all the fifteens and all the forty-fives, or *"quarter to* five."

Telling time IV   Now teach the overall idea behind the clock face. There are sixty minutes in every hour, one little mark for every minute. Have your child count from 1 to 60 as you move the hands around.

Then say you'd like to teach the child a shortcut so that he or she won't have to count up that high every time to find out what time it is. Set the clock down and teach the child how to count by fives, from 5 to 60. Then, move the clock around again and have the child point to each number and count by fives—3:05, 3:10, 3:15 and so on. (Say you know it's confusing that other numbers are on the clock, but they're there to tell the hours, which are even more important.)

Telling time V   Quiz your child on telling time by moving the clock hands to various times of day, asking him or her what time it is and telling the child what he or she usually does at that time of day. Introduce the concepts "a.m." and "p.m."—"after midnight" and "in the afternoon."

Telling time VI   With your child writing or connecting the dots, help him or her to record a basic family schedule of key times: "6:30 a.m.—we get up" and so on.

Calendars   Show your child how calendars use numbers to tell us what day it is. With your child, point to the numbers, 1 to 30 or 31, gradually teaching him or her to do it alone. Point out that the "teen numbers," like 13 or 14, have the "one" first, since they are in the "tens family." The twenties numbers have the "two" first and they are in the "twenties family" and so on. As you go along, point out "today" on the calendar, and next Saturday or a birthday, adding that numbers help us to remember these days.

Other household numbers   Ask your child to be a "number detective"—somebody who goes around the house looking for numbers on everyday items. Unless he or she finds exotic examples, stick with ones like these:

> The telephone. Explain that it takes seven numbers to dial a person's house or office and everybody has a different number.
> The washing machine or dryer. It has different stages of its cycle, using numbers.
> The blender, slow cooker or refrigerator. These have "gradations" of slower-faster, hotter-cooler and so on, shown by numbers.

Addresses   Ask your child how the mail carrier knows to deliver our mail to our house. (And make sure that he or she remembers your own address and other personal facts from Chapter Four: Basic Knowledge.) Do a lot of other people have our same address? Does anybody?

Then show your child your address book or list of

relatives' and friends' addresses. These numbers belong only to them, too.

Next, look in the telephone directory at all the different addresses and phone numbers. All of these provide good examples of the many important uses of numbers.

Cards   Teach your child to classify regular playing cards in number groups so that all the fours are in one pile, all the eights in another, etc. Cards use numbers, too. Once this goes well, play a game of Crazy Eights.

Money   Get a pile of pennies for your child to count. (More games on money are found in Chapter Eleven: The Basic Community and Chapter Fourteen: Fun Facts And How To Find Them.) Tell him or her that long ago people didn't have money. Instead, they used shells, jewels, even cows to pay each other for goods and services. Why might money have been invented? Why is it important to be able to count money?

Counting by twos   Begin this game by telling your child that some numbers are odd and some are even. With your fingers, illustrate the difference by showing that even numbers are the ones that can be divided into two equal parts. (If you have two children, this system can save you endless discussions over the division of household responsibilities and privileges. Just assign one child to the odd-numbered days and the other child to the even-numbered days.)

The next step is counting by twos, which teaches a little number flexibility and is even a good introduction to higher mathematics. Begin by writing down the numbers from 1 to 20. Have your child circle the 2, then every other number (4, 6, 8, 10, etc.). Explain that counting by twos means saying one number, then skipping the next one and so on.

More counting   Now do counting by fives and by tens, again by writing down the numbers and circling the right ones. Point out to your child that counting by fives gives you all numbers that end in 5 or 0, and counting by tens gives you all the first numbers in the number families.

Next, count backwards—10 or more, down to 0. (This can end in a "blast-off," with you lifting the child high off the ground. After all, this is cause for celebration; your child has been doing a little "subtraction.")

Numbers have names I   Show your child that numbers have names, too. Help him or her write out the words— "one," "two" and so on up to "fifteen."

Numbers have names II   As above, but continue up to thirty.

3 ✳ NUMBERS ARE MORE PLACES THAN YOU THINK, OR BE A BIG KID NUMBER DETECTIVE

Here your child can begin to understand *why* numbers are used in so many places. Numbers serve as a means of measurement and classification. They also can describe something so that it can't be confused with anything else. (Basic measuring games are found in Chapter Ten: Science Tricks.)

Home numbers measure I   Show your child the numbers on your thermostat. Explain how we choose a number—that is, a temperature—for our house. Then, in elementary terms, outline how this mechanism works.

You may want to say, "We adjust the thermostat, which makes the motor in the furnace work to heat or cool the house."

This is also a good time to discuss number temperature ranges. Explain to your child that ninety degrees is really hot, minus thirty degrees is very, very cold and so on, whatever ranges are common in your area. (Jump into Celsius and Fahrenheit differences only if you feel committed and if your child is ready.)

Home numbers measure II   Next, take your child on a brief tour of other numbers found around the home—the utility meter, the price markings on food containers in the kitchen, the ads showing prices in the newspaper and the numbers showing sizes on his or her clothing. Conduct this tour in just enough detail to give your child the idea that numbers measure many things for us, that big numbers signify more and that little numbers signify less.

Numbers away from home   On a shopping trip Mini-School, point out (and ask your child to read, if possible) numbers on grocery store items, other store price tags, gas pumps and license plates. Numbers are everywhere.

Numbers identify things   Ask your child why the government doesn't give anybody else our same license plate number. Convey the idea that numbers can identify something so that nobody gets it confused with anything else. Then, show your child other identifying numbers— your social security number, driver's license number and so on. Point out that these types of numbers are "long" or "big" so that there are enough numbers for everyone to have a different one.

Job numbers   Show your child how adults use numbers

at work. Bring home computer printouts, data sheets, mailing lists, legal citations, etc. Let your child find numbers on them that he or she knows. Then introduce the larger numbers, which fascinate most children.

Number facts   Explain to your child that sixty seconds equal one minute, twenty-four hours equal one day, seven days equal one week, thirty or thirty-one days equal one month (except for February); twelve inches equal one foot, three feet equal one yard; two pints equal one quart and sixteen ounces equal one pound (measure light items). Show each measure but don't worry about your child memorizing them all at once. The idea to convey is that numbers are used to measure just about everything.

4 ❋ USING NUMBERS, OR WHAT IS TWO PLUS TWO?

These activities teach basic number manipulation. Though most involve rote learning, they serve as a good foundation for a later, more sophisticated understanding of numbers. The are also sheer mental exercise and a lot of fun.

Write the numbers   Teach your child to write the numbers 1 through 10. Use the connect-the-dots approach explained for alphabet letters in Chapter Six: Pre-Writing. And remember to start with numbers using straight lines—like 1, 4, 5, 7, 9 and 10. They are easier for tiny fingers to cope with than those with curved lines. Point out to your child that just by putting these ten numbers together in various forms, he or she could write any number in the world. Then ask your child to tell you one huge number he or she would like to write.

Identify the numbers I   Write down any number, 1 through 10, and ask your child what it is. Do all of them.

Next, proceed to identifying 11 through 31, probably the hardest group because numbers like 12 and 21, and 13 and 31, are difficult to distinguish at first. (Please don't worry that your child has some learning disability if he or she tends to confuse them—this is normal.)

Identify the numbers II   Teach your child to identify the rest of the numbers through 99. Make sure to quiz him or her with the numbers out of their order and to repeat that the "twenties family" always starts with "two" and so on.

Biggies   Ask your child what huge numbers you should write for him or her. After a few of these, give the child a turn to write "biggies," with your help.

Point out as you go along that in "two-digit" or "two-place" numbers like 63 and 14, the 3 and 4 are in the "ones place" and the 6 and 1 are in the "tens place." Then mention that "hundreds" numbers like 189 and 257 have a "hundreds place," too, and bigger numbers have a "thousands place." This is very complicated and should be just told to your child, not really taught.

Adding with fingers   Ask your child to add "2 plus 2" and other simple sums, by counting the fingers you hold up. Make sure that he or she understands the words "plus," "equals," "adding" and "addition." And stress that when we add, we always get a bigger number than what we started with. Have your child add eight or ten "problems."

Subtracting with fingers   This is really even easier. "Five minus 2 equals 3" can be seen when your child folds back two of your five fingers. Point out the words "minus," "equals," "subtracting" and "subtraction." And stress that when we subtract, we "take away" an amount from the original number and so we always end up with a smaller number. Do eight or ten "problems."

Adding on paper   Once your child writes numbers well and has mastered simple addition and subtraction, have him or her write elementary, horizontal arithmetic problems, such as: 9 + 1 = ——. Have your child practice these without using his or her fingers.

This is easier if your child first makes a "number ladder"—a long, vertical list of the numbers from 1 (at the bottom) to 20 (at the top). Tell the child to find 9 on the ladder, then climb "one" more up the number ladder. Then have him or her record the answer. Always point out that in addition the result is always more, like "adding" icing to a cake.

Practice small sums such as: 2 + 3 = ——, 10 + 5 = ——, etc., often enough so your child can memorize many of them. (A small calculator, the kind where the child has to supply the answer, is good practice here and a lot of fun, too.)

Subtracting on paper   As above, but remember to illustrate only simple subtractions. Begin with something like: 9 − 1 = ——.

Again, use the "number ladder." Start with the 9, then have your child move "one" *down* the ladder. Subtraction is "taking away," like taking away food. So the result is always less.

Have your child practice solving and recording the answers to more small problems such as: 8 − 4 = ——, 20 − 1 = ——, etc. Remind him or her that a subtraction is a little like a sentence—one always has to start at the beginning.

Adding in columns   Explain to your child that for bigger numbers, it's much easier to use columns. Show him or her how to line up two-digit addition problems (where no "carrying" is necessary) such as:

$$\begin{array}{r} 12 \\ + \ 23 \\ \hline \end{array}$$

with the "ones places" under each other and the "tens places" under each other.

Then show your child the "shortcut"—all we have to do is add 2 plus 3 and write 5 under the "ones place," then add 1 plus 2 and write 3 under the "tens place." Presto—the answer is 35.

Do several like this.

Subtracting in columns   As above, but with subtraction problems that require no "borrowing." Practice several of them.

Multiplying I   Ask your child to add 2 plus 2 plus 2. Then explain that you can teach him or her a shortcut. It works only when you add numbers which are all the same.

Set out three different pairs of crayons or other small identical objects. Ask your child to pick up 2 crayons times 3—then count the total. Repeat the exercise with 3 times 3, 4 times 2, 3 times 1, 2 times 2 and other simple ones. Tell your child that this is "multiplication" and that big kids even memorize some of the answers so that they don't have to figure them out each time.

Multiplying II   Teach your child how to write multiplication problems using the following two methods:

$$2 \times 4 = 8$$
and
$$2 (4) = 8.$$

Then, with the crayons, teach some of the harder ones—3 times 0, 3 times 1, 4 times 0, 4 times 1 and so on. Explain that any number multiplied by 0 equals 0 and any number multiplied by 1 equals the original number. Also stress that in multiplication it doesn't matter which number you start with.

Dividing   Set out crayons again (or other small objects)—perhaps eight of them. Then, ask your child to divide them into two groups, so that each group contains the same number of crayons. You have just done a division problem.

$$8 \div 2 = 4$$
or
$$2 \overline{)8}^{\,4}$$

(Write it both ways.)

Then ask your child to divide the eight crayons into four groups, with each group containing the same number of crayons. Also illustrate this problem on paper.

These are difficult but enjoyable number tricks. So, do a few more together. And then just mention that division is the opposite of multiplication.

Numbers in other languages   Most children like to be able to count to ten in another language. *Sesame Street* specializes in Spanish. You can review that and/or choose another language, just for fun.

5 ✷ GETTING A SENSE OF NUMBERS, OR THINKING WITH NUMBERS

As we discussed at the beginning of this Mini-School area, the manipulation of numbers is fun for children, but it is not the same as thinking in terms of them or understanding how they structure our thinking. Although this is an advanced concept for your preschooler, he or she can take a step toward it by learning to appreciate time scales and size scales.

You might begin with some commercial conceptual number equipment. Many preschools and some toy stores have equipment like Cuisenaire rods, various color-coded ones to tens to one-hundreds sticks, as well as Montessori and Montessori-like toys. Look at them and consider buying a set or making your own version at home. (Or do what I do—ask the children's preschool teacher to please stress these games with your children, if they tend to get more language than numbers work at home.)

Guesstimates   To stress thinking in terms of numbers, fill a small jar with M & M's, small marshmallows or other uniformly sized objects. Ask your child to look very carefully and then guess how many are in there. Hint: look at the jar part by part—there may be about eight in the top half, so the bottom half probably has about eight, too. So the "guesstimate" would be sixteen.

Next, use larger jars and take turns guessing. Then,

ask your child to count the contents and see who was closer.

Next, try to figure out how many of your child's "Big Wheels" would fit in the kitchen, how many apples would fit in your child's pillowcase and so on. Check out some of them.

Time spans   Give your child a calendar and ask him or her to count the days remaining until Christmas, until his or her next birthday or until other key holidays that occur in the not too distant future. Explain that our planet Earth has 365 days in every year (except leap year with 366) because that's how long it takes our planet to go around the sun, and that each planet has a different number of days in its year.

Schedules, if you have one or a semblance of one, can help teach about time spans, too. Have your child write down when you usually eat breakfast, lunch and dinner. Calculate together, using subtraction, how many hours between these and other key domestic events.

Infinity   No one seems to really understand this concept, but children often ask, "What is the biggest number?" Show them the symbol ∞ and say "infinity." It just means that numbers go on forever. We could keep on counting and always have another number.

Chapter Thirteen: Writing

The learning games in this area will help your child learn to write, provided that he or she has mastered the activities in Chapter Six: Pre-Writing. The activities here proceed from a review of all the letters by the connect-the-dots method to writing the whole alphabet; to writing favorite names; to writing special words, labels and lists; to creating a short book; and even to some quite adult writing rules and refinements.

Like virtue, writing is, in a sense, its own reward. Imagine the sense of achievement and pride your child will feel at being able to write his or her own name, "Happy Birthday" or "I love you" on a piece of paper. And imagine the sense of independence your child will feel when he or she can make a license plate for a favorite truck, a "keep out" sign for a room door or a list of favorite toys to take along on the family vacation. In so doing, your child will have achieved half of literacy (reading is the other half)—a level attained, unfortunately, by less than half the world's population.

To boost motivation, show your child how *you* use writing. At home, mention it when you are making a grocery list ("so that we won't forget the grapes") and offer to jot down a message to the sitter or preschool

183

teacher that has been on the child's mind ("Now Mrs. Jensen will know for sure."). Also, you and your spouse should bring home handwritten projects from work for a family "show and tell."

Writing provides extra academic motivation, too. Your child may become quite curious about and even adept at spelling. You can encourage this by saying things like, "It's time for the b-a-t-h, bath," or by spelling out potential birthday presents or other "secrets" to your spouse in the child's presence.

These games are all for preschoolers, though they will be quite difficult for some in this age group. Small muscle development is required for writing, and it proceeds at quite different rates in children. So don't rush your child—and make sure he or she has had ample chance to practice scribbling while holding the writing implement properly.

Remember that the games move, roughly, from easier to harder, within a game group and from one group to another. Choose five minutes worth of activities for each Mini-School.

1 ✳ REVIEW ALL THE LETTERS, OR CONNECT THE DOTS

To launch your child into solo writing, have him or her review all the letters with the connect-the-dot method explained in Chapter Six: Pre-Writing.

Dot it up I   Ask your child which alphabet letter he or she would like to write with the connect-the-dots method. Make sure that he or she eventually completes the entire uppercase alphabet. At this point, don't be too concerned with the letters sitting properly on a straight line. But do see that your child follows the sequence of letter formations that you do (e.g., for "d," make the straight line first, then connect the semicircle).

Dot it up II   As above, but for the lowercase letters.

2 ✳ THE WHOLE ALPHABET, OR YOU DID IT ALL YOURSELF

These games ask your child to write the letters all by him- or herself. Don't use regular lined paper at this point—the writing space is too narrow. Instead, ask your child to draw rough horizontal lines across plain white paper and use those.

Your name   With no dots to connect, help your child to write his or her own name, uppercase letter first, then the rest with lowercase letters. (Teachers generally prefer this to all uppercase letters.) Those with short names can do their last names, too!

Alphabet soup I   Now, help your child practice writing any uppercase alphabet letter he or she chooses. If you suggest any, begin with those that use straight lines (they are easier).

Alphabet soup II   Finish the uppercase ones.

Alphabet soup III   Ask your child to write approximately half of the lowercase letters, again remembering that the ones with straight lines are easier.

Alphabet soup IV   Finish the remaining lowercase letters.

The whole bit   Review the whole alphabet, both upper- and lowercase letters. If your child has forgotten any letters, you can write those on another piece of paper for him or her to look at and then to imitate (no longer use the connect-the-dots method).

Then teach your child which letters sit on the line, which hang below and which grow up tall. Tape the results on the refrigerator!

3 ✳ Names, or That's All of Us

The names of people we love are beautiful to us. (And seeing your child write them is even more beautiful.)

That's us   Ask your child to write the first names of his or her favorite people. Make sure that each begins with an uppercase letter and then contains all the lowercase letters. And remind the child to write each name on the (very wide) lines.

4 ✳ Special Writing Projects, or You're Literate Now

This set of games is a package of rewards for writing and will reinforce your child's interest in his or her new skill. The games here, especially, should be repeated periodically because most young children don't write very often and they can easily forget some individual letters.

Your choice   Ask your child what words he or she would like to write, one by one. You may end up with "dinosaur" and "marshmallow" or "car" and "Mom." Help your child's spelling skills simultaneously by asking him or her what letter "comes next" before actually writing it.

By this time you are teaching spelling as well as writing, so start to teach a few basic spelling tricks such as:

the sound "ur" can be spelled as "ir," "er" or "ur" but is most often "er"

short words with long vowel sounds in the middle often end in a "silent e"

the sound "ee" can be spelled "ie," "ee," "ea" or "y"

Labeling   On small pieces of paper, your child can make labels for anything in the house from "sofa" to "my bed." (This will help your child's reading ability, too.)

Any list   Ask your child to suggest any type of list he or she might like to write. It could be a list of Christmas presents, grocery or drugstore items, bad table manners (ours is posted on the refrigerator and functions as a humorous reminder), thoughts for the preschool teacher or sitter, favorite animals or necessities to take along on a trip. These can be posted on what's left of the refrigerator door, or kept in the child's special secret drawer.

As in the previous game, have the child help with the spelling and drop a spelling hint or two along the way. Also stress how nice it is that we can write—so that we don't have to try to remember *everything*.

A book I   An illustrated book is a perfect present for a parent or grandparent. Your child could write a "Happy Birthday Book" with a few simple wishes for the recipient's day, complete with pictures. Or he or she could do a longer story about a "Walk in the Park" or "My Favorite Vehicles."

Help your child choose a title to write on the cover, along with his or her name. Then help your child spell the words in the first few pages of the book. Remember to leave space for illustrations.

A book II   Finish writing the book, add illustrations and staple or tape the masterpiece together. These are our family specialty. For Christmas presents we even let our children tape in snapshots of themselves on some of the pages. (For an even more ambitious book project, see Chapter Twenty-Six: Make a Family Book.)

5 ✳ WRITING REFINEMENTS, OR GROWN-UP WRITING

Before undertaking these games, make sure your child is writing letters proficiently, spelling many words and also reading well. There is no point in teaching refinements such as capitalization, punctuation, special marks like dollar signs or typing before the basic skills have been mastered.

Capitalization   Open one of your child's simpler books and ask him or her to find some uppercase letters. Then ask if there are more uppercase or more lowercase letters on that page. Where are the uppercase letters most often found? Show the child that there is one at the beginning of each new sentence and at the beginning of every person's name.

More capitalization   Open one of the child's slightly more complicated books to a page using quotation marks and, if possible, place names. Ask your child to find an uppercase or "capital" letter that is *not* starting a sentence or a person's name. Then explain that places, days of the week and months of the year begin with uppercase letters, too—and so do "quotations," what someone is saying in the book.

Punctuation   Show your child the following punctuation marks. Ask him or her to find them in a book and then write each on a piece of paper:

> a comma (between words in a list or between
>   two ideas in a sentence)
> a question mark (for a question)
> a period (at the end of a sentence)
> an exclamation mark or point (means "wow")
> an apostrophe (to show that someone owns
>   something or to point out where a letter
>   is missing)
> quotation marks (to show what somebody
>   said)

Help your child make up a sentence that would use each of these punctuation marks if we wrote it down.

Special marks   Teach your child the dollar sign and the cents symbol by showing grocery markings.

Then teach the basic names of other special marks like the triple dot (. . .) and ampersand (&). (This is especially fun if your child can find them on a typewriter.)

Writing fractions   Show your child how to write fractions two ways—e.g., ¼ and $\frac{1}{4}$

Typing   Before your child can write well, a typewriter is a crutch. Once he or she can write, though, it's a reward and a unique treat. Let him or her type any and all letters to get used to the machine. Then ask your child to type his or her own name and a few other simple words.

Small writing   Once your child can write proficiently, have him or her practice writing small enough to fit between the lines of a regular elementary school writing tablet (not as narrowly drawn as those for adults). Now you're like an elementary school kid!

Chapter Fourteen: Fun Facts and How to Find Them

WHAT, WHY AND WHO

The learning games here are designed to intrigue your child, to interest him or her in finding out more about the world and to suggest some ways to do so. Topics covered include household machines, outer space, basic biology, money, your own field of expertise, current events and how to locate needed information. (More basic introductions to the first four topics can be found in Chapter Four: Basic Knowledge, Chapter Seven: Daily Life and Chapter Eleven: The Basic Community.)

These subjects are intended to be interesting in themselves, but the most basic goal of these games is to further your child's general love for and curiosity about learning. Some of the games convey information, while others show your child how to find out more information. Your child has learned by now that you, your spouse and possibly a sitter and preschool teacher are good sources of information. But he or she needs sources beyond these individuals to answer questions that you may not be able to answer, such as, "What was the biggest dinosaur?" or, "Why don't those heavy-looking rain clouds just fall down to the ground?" You can, however, show your child how to look for the answers. And you can tell your child that there are many questions that no one understands completely; scientists are still studying many of them.

These games are appropriate for older preschool children, those who can read or almost read. They are also appropriate for you—you may end up learning along with your child (I did!).

1 ✳ HOUSEHOLD MACHINES, OR WHAT MAKES THAT WASHING MACHINE WASH?

This set of games will teach your child about some of the appliances and machines we all take for granted. They can be investigated in different ways—by peering at them while they work, by physically taking them apart or by researching them in an encyclopedia (at home or in the library for a Saturday Mini-School).

Power   Begin by walking around the house with your child, teaching him or her the names of all the appliances that get their power from electricity. (How do you know? Look for a plug.) Next, look for battery-powered mechanisms (including toys).

Then find, if you have them, the natural-gas, solar-powered and oil-powered appliances. And show the child where all these power sources enter the appliance and how they get into the house or car.

How it works   Have your child choose an appliance to discover (very basically) how it works. Peer inside, open it up, take it apart (if you dare, perhaps only very minimally). If neither of you knows how it works, look it up in a home-repair manual or in an encyclopedia.

What you are essentially doing here is providing a basic two- or three-sentence explanation, teaching how people find out information like this *and* boosting your child's curiosity. (If your child chooses the car, you might add, for example, "We have a *gasoline-powered* car. Scientists haven't really figured out yet how to make the best battery for an *electric* car, but they are building them. You might want to work on that more when you grow up.") Or you might ask your child, "How many of your favorite machines use a wheel—on the outside *or* on the inside?" Stress that there is still plenty left to learn in the world.

2 ✳ OUTER SPACE, OR NOBODY COULD EVER COUNT ALL THE STARS

Here your child can learn some basic fun facts about outer space and intensify his or her sense of wonder at the same time. Anything that especially intrigues the child can be followed up in game 7, "How To Find Out Things."

Names I   Find a huge piece of paper or tape smaller ones together to help your child draw the sun and the planets. Have him or her draw a yellow sun in the middle and label it. Then, in concentric circles (forget the problems of scale), add the planets Mercury, Venus, Earth and Mars.

Names II   Have your child add the asteroids, Jupiter, Saturn, Uranus, Neptune and Pluto. Next, add our moon as a small circle near Earth.

While all this is going on, throw in a random fact or two about some of the planets. (Mercury is so hot it would sizzle us in a second. Venus always has a cloudy sky. Earth is our planet. Mars is full of reddish rocks. Jupiter is only swirling thick clouds, probably without a

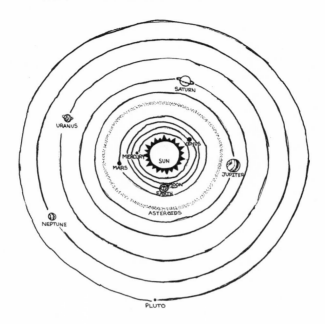

solid core. Saturn has dozens of rings. Neptune is so cold that ice wouldn't melt even in summer. Uranus has a few faint rings. And Pluto is just a hunk of frozen gas.) If there is time, act out with your child a rocket trip to his or her favorite planet.

Stars   For an outdoor, nighttime Mini-School, begin by telling your child that our sun is just a very close star, a "nuclear furnace" so hot that we would burn to a crisp if we even got near it. Then point out that all the stars in the sky at night are suns too, but they look tiny because they are very, very far away.

Next, ask your child to find some big star groups or to identify the shapes which some star groups take. Find the Big Dipper, as one example.

Mention to your child, too, that no one has ever counted the stars or knows if there are any planets around all those other suns. "But you might want to be an astronomer and study them when you grow up."

The weather   In closer, not outer, space "meteorologists" are still learning about the weather, too. Tell your child that lightning is "wild electricity," thunder is the sound lightning makes, wind blows because the earth is spinning around in the sky with hot and cold air mixing together, rain is water around a bit of dust falling down from the clouds, snow is freezing rain, and hail is ice from clouds in colder air.

Mention that no two snowflakes are alike because each one consists of millions of tiny ice crystals arranging themselves around a tiny bit of dust in different ways.

Encourage your child to ask you questions about the weather. Those that you don't know can be researched in another Mini-School. Or, also in a later Mini-School, you can help your child phone one of the local TV weather announcers and ask the question.

3 ✳ Basic Biology, or Where Do People Come From Before They Are Born?

These games can be as scanty or as full of information as you wish—but remember not to overwhelm your child with information. It is better to give short explanations and let him or her ask more questions. (Sometimes a little is all a child wants to know.)

Body parts   Review with your child the more difficult parts of our bodies (from Chapter One: Basic Things).

Then add others, such as:

temples	instep	spine
sole of the	appendix	other more
foot		exotic
		internal
		organs

Tell your child that everything was there when he or she was born. But it keeps growing.

Birth   To ascertain what your child understands, ask him or her how people are born. Straighten out common misconceptions. Many children believe that babies grow in the mother's stomach (where they catch part of the food) and that the father has no share in the project. Explain that half of the baby's body cells came from the dad and half from the mom, that the baby grows in the uterus and that it is born through the vagina.

Death   By age three, all children begin to think about death—so discussing it together will reassure, not frighten, your child. Begin by pointing out a dead bird or even a dead bug or leaf. Then listen to your child's questions. Stress that everything gets old and dies— leaves on the trees in fall, birds and even people. Emphasize that people usually die only when they are very old. Be open to questions about where they go, what happens to their clothes, whether you might die and so on, and give lots of reassurance about how *very, very rare* death is for children or their parents.

4 ✳ MONEY, OR CLOTHES AND TOYS DON'T GROW ON TREES

The games here should deepen your child's sophistication about money (see Chapter Eleven: The Basic Community and Chapter Twelve: Numbers for earlier activities along these lines). Without worrying your child about dire poverty, tell your preschooler that people work to earn money so that they can buy clothes, food, housing, toys and cars.

What costs what   Start in the kitchen by asking your child to read aloud some of the prices marked on the grocery products. Then, take your child on a "money tour" of the house, where he or she can ask you, roughly, how much things cost.

Earning it   Take turns making a list (oral or written) of all the adult jobs you both can think of. Have your child interrupt you to ask about any that interest him or her. In each case, explain the employee's duties, the approximate salary and the good and bad aspects of that job. (Remain respectful and nonsexist!)

5 ✳ OUR EXPERTISE, OR WHAT MOM AND DAD ARE ESPECIALLY GOOD AT

These games are intended to draw on your own expertise, your knowledge gained from work and hobbies. You can probably play dozens of games based on these, in formats like those suggested below.

Mom's special stuff   Choose your job or special hobby, and show your child a little bit about how you do it. What reading, writing, arithmetic, verbal and listening skills does it require? What is the result of your work? (A trip to Mom's computer programming job, for example, would be an especially good idea here.)

Dad's special stuff   Do the same in this case. A trip to Dad's job or a "guest day" with your spouse as Mini-School teacher would be especially valuable. Hearing about and/or participating in Dad's hobbies, from collecting rocks to trimming bushes, can teach a lot.

6 ✳ CURRENT EVENTS, OR WHAT HAPPENED TODAY?

These games provide an introduction to the variety of information in today's newspaper and on today's newscast, an area more fascinating to most young children than you may realize. They are also important learning tools because they teach children how to get information about specific events and, quite often, current ideas. (Earlier activities, focusing on what makes up a newspaper, are found in Chapter Eight: Visual Information and in Chapter Eleven: The Basic Community.)

Today's paper   Page through today's newspaper with your child, focusing this time on the news content. Point out interesting stories, summarizing them for your child. Answer lots of questions. And mention the different parts of the paper—ads, headlines, comics and so on.

Today's TV news   Watch the local or national news alone with your child. Translate each story into something within the child's experience and answer lots of questions. (Don't be surprised if you encounter some strange misconceptions. Our three-year-old had heard that nuclear power plants could be dangerous. When we were listening to a report about some minor developments at a nearby plant, he commented, "I'm glad I don't have to water that nuclear power plant.")

7 ✳ How to Find Out Things, or Be an Information Detective

Here the activities demonstrate for your child some of the different sources we can use to find information. Most, if not all, will require parental help. Remember one or two unanswerable questions from your child and, at some point, spend a weekend Mimi-School looking them up.

TV listings   The TV listings can be your child's first reference work. Teach him or her how to find the day of the week, the time of day, the channel and the name of a show in the listings. Then ask, "What's on Saturday at 11 A.M. on Channel 2?"

Point out that a TV guide is an example of something we don't read the whole way through. We use it "as a reference, to look things up."

Encyclopedias   When your child wants to know the name of the largest dinosaur and why they are all dead now, investigate the answers with him or her in a children's encyclopedia.

Ask your child to find the "D" volume for "Dinosaurs" and show, briefly, how the volume is alphabetized. Then, while your child looks at the pictures and perhaps reads a bit of the article, you locate the answer and show the child where you found it.

Books for Reference   Although any fact book or compendium of information would work here, some of our most interesting Mini-Schools along these lines have been spent with one of the *Charlie Brown's Book of Questions and Answers* series. Let your child choose a chapter in a book like this, and you both can look through it, reading tidbits of interesting information. (This can be done at the library or at home.)

Chapter Fifteen: Reading

The learning games in this area will help your child to become a reader. They include flash card reading, rhyme reading, reading street signs and other signs, reading words here and there, kitchen reading, reading whole books and adult reading.

A child who can read is one who has found as many new worlds as there are books in the library. The achievement, whenever it comes, is actually almost magical. And the pride your child will feel cannot be exaggerated.

Even at the first threshold of "whole book literacy" your child may feel motivated enough to concentrate for an hour over a Dr. Seuss Beginner's Book—and to finally finish it. He or she may check out an armful of library books and read them, one by one, immediately, curious about everything from Paris taxis to Utah dinosaurs.

When I began to hold Mini-School, for example, I had no intention of urging my children to read. I wanted only to prepare them well for school, with skills like those in Chapter Five: Pre-Reading. So I didn't push them to read or encourage them to guess at words (a bad habit, anyway). But when my first child kept begging to "read in Mini today," I decided not to hold her back. At four and one-half years old, she had just made up her mind to read books. And she did. (Then I became excited enough to buy her a new Dr. Seuss Beginner Book for every one she learned to read. After ten of those, a hefty investment which could have been avoided by checking out a secret supply of library books, she was ready for some of the other children's books we already had around.) She was launched into a fluency that has given her a sense of achievement, joy and excitement.

Having a literate child can create problems, though, which are worth considering beforehand. The first possibility is that a parent *could* stop reading books *to* that child simply because the child can read alone. Please do not cease this activity. The warm, friendly atmosphere of being read to fosters closeness as well as additional learning.

The second problem for your child may come later, at elementary school. Ask your school now if any special provision is made in kindergarten for children who already know how to read. If you can, mention other kindergarten children you know who can read, or nearby preschool programs which already teach pre-reading and reading skills, and the background provided to many children by *Sesame Street* and *Electric Company*. Speak with or check on all the district's kindergarten teachers so that you may request the most receptive one. One may be truly delighted to have a reader in class and take time to challenge your child. Or, if necessary, consider a private kindergarten.

All this is worth the trouble, I suspect, even for very busy parents. If you tend to agree, proceed through the following games and choose a five-minute activity for every Mini-School.

1 ✳ Flash Cards, or Touch That Sofa

The games here use a variety of homemade personal flash cards, adapted to your home and your child's interests. (Of course, you could use commercial flash cards instead.) The games begin with a relatively simple, motivating series of individual words. They are appropriate when your child is starting to sound out words, however slowly.

Do it   On pieces of paper the size of 5″ by 7″ index cards (preferably stiff and even colored paper, for fun), write, one per card, simple action words—e.g., hop, jump, walk, run, gallop, crawl, squat and lie down—all in lowercase letters (the way your child will be seeing them in books).

Spread them out on the floor. Then ask your child to choose them, one by one, in any order. The child sounds out each word, then performs each action.

Touch it   Ask your child what objects in the house we should use to make "object flash cards." Then (according to the suggestions in the "do it" game above) make cards for the objects—chair, TV, block sofa and so on. (If your child requests a couple of hard ones like "magazine rack," that's all right, too.)

Again, spread them out—let your child choose them in any order and then run to touch the object he or she has just read.

2 ✳ Rhyme Reading, or Just Change One Sound

A treat for any beginning reader, each of these games is arranged around a set of similar words. They are a pretty good yardstick of how close your child really is to true reading. They are easy if your child is ready, not at all easy if he or she is not. And, if your child has been watching *Electric Company* long enough, they may be just the last necessary boost toward true reading skills.

Vowel sounds I   Make a list of similar words like those below, printed carefully in horizontal lines so that the similarities are easy to point out. Then have your child sound out each word, one by one. Point out which sounds are similar. For example, in the first line you can say, "Each word has a short 'a' for 'a' and a 'tuh' on the end."

rat, hat, mat, bat, sat, pat, fat (short "a")
hit, bit, sit, fit, pit (short "i")
take, lake, bake, make, rake (long "a")

Vowel sounds II   As above, but with:

boo, woo, coo, moo, too (double "o")
ball, wall, hall, mall, call, fall (broad "a")
like, bike, Mike, dike, hike, pike (long "i")

Vowel sounds III   As above, but with:

bet, wet, net, met, pet, get, let, set (short "e")
more, sore, bore, tore, wore (long "o")
weed, seed, feed, heed, need (double "e")

Vowel sounds IV   As above, but with:

bread, read, lead ("ea"—the "a" is silent)
mop, hop, pop, bop, top (short "o")

up, pup, cup, sup (short "u")
pure, cure, lure (long "u")

Vowel sounds V   As above, but with:

book, look, took, nook, cook ("oo")
sour, hour ("ou")
sow, window, low, mow (one of the two
    different "ow" sounds)
wow, pow, cow, now

Vowel sounds VI   As above, but with:

funny, sunny, bunny (the "y's" "ee" sound)
yogurt, yellow, yum (the "y's" "yuh" sound)
pay, say, hay, pray, gay ("ay")

Special consonant diphthongs   As above, but with:

think, thing, thump, thank ("th")
chip, chin, cheer, chirp ("ch")
shut, sheep, ship, shine ("sh")
where, when, whine, why ("wh")

Special consonant diphthongs II   As above, but with:

stand, stale, stir, stare ("st")
slurp, slime, slat, sleep ("sl")
cry, creek, crank, creep ("cr")
gray, grin, gripe, grape ("gr")

Special sounds   As above, but with:

quack, quick, queen, queer ("qu")

phone, telephone, phonograph ("ph")
vacation, position, friction, section ("tion")

3 ✳ STREET SIGNS AND OTHER SIGNS, OR STOP

When your child can read simple words quickly enough, show him or her how reading helps us get important information quickly.

Street signs   On a Mini-School walk or car or bus ride through the neighborhood, read the street signs to your child, including everything from "Stop" to "Yield" to "I-94." Explain the graphic symbols for curved road, etc., as they appear. Then let your child read the rest of the signs you encounter.

Home signs   With your child, make information signs such as "keep out" for a child's door or "hideout" for a favorite corner. Then have the child read them back to you and put them where they belong.

4 ✳ READ A LITTLE, OR WORDS HERE AND THERE

This game encourages your child to sound out and read words without the consistent sounds found in previous games.

Familiar words   Write down, for your child, familiar words such as "Mom," "Dad," the child's name, "Exit," "*Sesame Street,*" whatever you think the child has seen often. Have the child read them.

A familiar book   Read a familiar book to your child, stopping after every few sentences for the child to sound out one of the words. The book need not have a simple vocabulary because you will be reading most of the words anyway. But your child will feel as though he or she has partly "read the book."

5 ✻ POSTCARDS, OR READ IT, IT'S YOURS

Other reading boosters are postcards sent by a grand-parent or some you have hidden under your child's pillow. You can even use old picture postcards and letters, if you like, taping a new message on the back.

Read it   Write a simple message such as, "Dear Erik, You are a nice boy. Love, Mom." Tell your child that you have hidden today's Mini-School under his or her pillow or in his or her shoe. The child finds it, reads it and keeps it.

6 ✻ KITCHEN READING, OR IS THAT WHEAT GERM OR BRAN?

This game capitalizes on all the interesting words found in the kitchen. Make sure to start with the simpler ones.

What is it?   Point out the main word in a forest of words and graphics on the front of a cereal box or wherever you can find relatively simple words. Ask your child to read it, making sure that he or she is not guessing. Gradually let your child find the main words and read even more of the label.

7 ✻ WHOLE BOOKS, OR I READ IT MYSELF

Once it becomes a possible dream, your child can

read a simple children's story all the way through. It can be a familiar book, as long as the child doesn't know every word by heart.

Your own book   Have your child dictate a story to you. Write it down. Then help the child read it back to you, with the child doing most of the reading.

Regular book I   Choose a fairly simple book. Your child should read and sound out all the words on every other page, alternating with you.

Regular book II   Choose a simple book for your child to read all the way through, alone, with your help only for words that are especially difficult to sound out.

Regular book III   Let your child choose any book from his or her collection, or even a new library book, to read from beginning to end in one or more Mini-School sessions.

8 ✳ GROWN-UP READING, OR YOU'RE LIKE MOM AND DAD

These games are a challenge for any child. Don't begin them until your child is an experienced reader—otherwise the experience may be discouraging.

Newspaper headlines   Pick up today's paper and ask your child to read some of the simpler headlines to you. Explain and help as necessary.

Magazine ads   As above, but with some of the simpler, flashier magazine advertisements.

Toy catalogs   Ask your child to choose a couple of toys to read about. One of them might make a good Christmas or birthday present.

Weird typefaces   See if your child can decipher some of the more unusual typefaces or styles found in consumer magazines or store signs.

Label reading   Have your child read some of the complicated parts of food labels. Point out that this is how adults discover what's in the food we buy.

Handwriting   Write the upper- and lowercase alphabets in a reasonably clear script or find printed examples. Then help your child read each letter, pointing out that these are very hard but that the secret is to try to ignore the "glide marks" that would attach the letter to the ones before and after.

Mirror writing   To be even more exotic, find a copy of *Alice In Wonderland* and show your child what "mirror writing" is. It looks like gibberish, but hold it up and presto—reading is even more magical now!

Part II: Family Creativity Time Sessions

Chapter Sixteen: What If?

The creativity sessions in this area ask your whole family to explore what would happen if something we take for granted were missing, or if we looked different, or if the world were quite different in some other way.

Their purpose is to encourage all family members to see the world in a new light, to explore new possibilities, to challenge their expectations and generally to open their minds and imaginations. Some of the ideas your child or children offer may sound like something which occurred in earlier cultures. If so, point this out, adding that early people were creative, too.

Choose five minutes worth of activities for each Family Creativity Time session—in other words, one or two questions from any of the sections below. Remember not to judge or evaluate anyone's responses. Everyone participates and anything goes!

1 ✳ WHAT IF SOMETHING WERE MISSING?

What would we do if . . .

there were no clothes?
there were no rules for children?

there were no roofs?
there were no schools?

there were no laws for
adults?

there were no rugs or
carpets?

there were no cars or
trucks?

there were no grocery
stores?

there was no electricity?

there were no animals?

there was no sun?

there were no
telephones?

nobody could talk?

nobody could walk?

there were no
washing
machines?

anything else?

2 ✳ WHAT IF WE LOOKED DIFFERENT?

What would we do if . . .

we had no thumbs?

we had no hair?

we had roller skates
instead of feet?

we had webbed feet like
ducks?

we had only one arm?

we had only one
leg?

we had no noses?

people were all
nocturnal, like
the owls?

we had four eyes
(two on the
back of our
heads)?

anything else?

3 ✳ WHAT IF THE WORLD WERE WEIRDER?

What would we do if . . .

trees could eat regular
food?

people could fly but
not walk?

dogs could talk?

nobody ever died?

something else grew
on trees, rather
than leaves?

candy grew on the
ground instead
of grass?

everything were a
    different color?
it rained something else
    instead of water?
people were born
    old and got
    younger every
    year?

gravity pulled everything
    up instead of down?
nobody ever got
    mad or sad?
anything else?

Chapter Seventeen: Name It

The creativity sessions in this area encourage your family to provide a brand new name for a common object or to create new words for unusual objects or phenomena.

Again, their purpose is to stretch the mind, provide some good family laughs and encourage a playful attitude toward objects and words.

Choose five minutes worth of creative activities—probably one or two of the examples below—for the whole family to do together. Accept any response—anything goes.

1 ❋ NAME A NEW KIND OF . . .

strawberry ice cream	soap
lemon ice cream	toothpaste
blueberry ice cream	deodorant
chocolate ice cream	shampoo
lemon pie	finger paint
butterscotch cake	TV set
granola cereal	something else

2 ✳   Make Up a New Word for Something or Somebody That Is . . .

A cross between . . .

an elephant and a
    grasshopper (e.g.,
    "elehopper" or
    "grass-stomper")
a dog and a dragon
a canary and a tricycle
a library and a gas station

a drugstore and a fish
    market
a book and a record

a person and a lion

a person and a fish
a train and a car
a boat and an
    airplane
a parent and a sitter

anything and
    anything

At the same time . . .

happy and sad
mad and yelling
fun and exciting
crying and shouting
hopping and jumping

grouchy and sick

whining and crying
snowing and raining
hot and humid
windy and rainy
any other
    combination

Chapter Eighteen: I Wish

The creativity sessions here prompt your family members to explore their imaginations so they can momentarily become animals, people in other jobs or something completely different, such as a cloud or a tree. They encourage everyone to project beyond themselves—to see, hear, listen and feel as someone or something else. These imaginative exercises are the beginning of acting—so ask everyone to "act it out." They also serve to promote understanding and sympathy for others. They may, too, uncover fears in your children which you can all discuss and probably allay. If you like, you can throw in a few fun facts about what an animal really eats or what an electrician really does. But stop if this begins to dampen the general exuberance of the moment; the atmosphere here should be one where "anything goes."

Choose five minutes worth of activities—in other words, one or two of the examples listed below. The whole family should take turns acting out each one.

1 ✳ I WISH I WERE AN ANIMAL

What would you do if you woke up one morning and discovered that you were an animal? What would you eat? Where would you sleep? Would you decide to wear clothes? What would seem strange to you? What would you think about if you were:

an elephant?	an anteater?
a cat?	a robin?
a squirrel?	a monkey?
a lion?	a dragon?
a turtle?	a dinosaur?
a giant bumblebee?	any animal?
a dog?	your favorite stuffed animal?

End the session with each family member walking around the room as his or her favorite animal.

2 ✳ I WISH I HAD THIS JOB

What would you do if you suddenly found yourself in a new, adult job? What tools would you use? What would you wear? How would you feel? How would you act if you got mad and could do *anything* to show your anger (a lawyer might throw ice cream at a judge, for example)? Choose from the following jobs:

a construction worker	a grocery store checkout person
a mail carrier	a dancing teacher
a lawyer	a plumber
an ice cream factory worker	a garbage collector
a teacher	a restaurant cook
a doctor	a mom
a toy maker	a dad
an electrician	a grandma

a TV journalist
a TV actor who plays the
    part of Kermit the
    Frog, Miss Piggy,
    etc.

a grandpa
anything else

An alternative way to play is to have each family member pantomime a job and have the others guess what it is.

3 ✳ I WISH I WERE SOMETHING COMPLETELY DIFFERENT

How would you feel and what would you see if you were:

a cloud?
a tree?

a moving van?
our house?
a bird?
a refrigerator?
a toilet?
a TV set?
the wind?
our garbage bag?
an ice cream cone?
a skyscraper?

a piece of bread?
a grocery store
    conveyor belt?
a bathtub?
a pillow?
a toy block?
a sidewalk?
a doll?
a tummy?
a piece of clay?
a tooth?
anything?

Chapter Nineteen: Story Recipes

WHAT AND WHY

The creativity sessions in this area ask your whole family to invent a story about a very bad child, a peculiar family, any three objects, a dream, a picture, the end of parents or bizarre foods. Each of these "story recipes" can be used many times, for more than one Family Creativity Time session.

Creating stories encourages family members to put together a whole creative project, with the minimal constraint that it hang together in some way. The subjects are designed to loosen inhibitions on thinking and lead to surrealistic details (which is what you will get from a toddler or younger preschooler). In getting the story started, try not to provide too much direction—after all, "anything goes."

Choose one of the story recipes below for your five-minute Family Creativity Time session. Each family member can take a turn telling a brief story on that subject, or you all may take turns adding a sentence or two at a time (the "family potboiler" method).

1 ✳ ONCE UPON A TIME THERE WAS
A VERY BAD KID

These stories are what I call "children's own pornography," where your child or children can exult in what they can imagine.

Before you begin, emphasize the following points:

We call this child a "very bad kid" because we don't distinguish between boys and girls (this way, no one gets the idea that sex determines behavior).

We aren't bad like this kid. We all have bad thoughts—sometimes we'd like to throw each other out the window—and that's okay. We aren't bad because we don't *do* these things; we would never do them.

We all do naughty things sometimes but nothing like this child who does *everything* bad *all* the time.

Start off with something like this:

> "Once upon a time the Very Bad Kid went to the grocery store and threw ten raw eggs at a nice old lady. The grocery store manager said that the kid had to leave. But the kid just laughed, opened a carton of milk and poured it over the manager's head." What else did the Very Bad Kid do?

2 ✳ A Day in the Life of the Goofy Family

Start off with something like this (along the lines of one of our favorite children's books, *The Stupids Step Out)*:

> "Once upon a time there was a goofy family. When they got up in the morning, they ate dinner right away. Then they put on their bathings suits and went to work and to school." What did they do next?

3 ✳ A Story About Three Things

One family member at a time chooses any three things to put in the middle of the floor (a truck, Mom's purse and a drum, for example). Then you each tell any story incorporating those three items.

With older children, use four or five objects, including some that can't be physically there (Dad's car, a lion, a spoon, the sun and a toy airplane, for example).

4 ✳ What I Wish I Would Dream Tonight

Begin by explaining that in dreams you can put anything in any time or place. For example, you could dream that your child's preschool teacher lived in the family's bathtub when he or she was a baby. Further emphasize that dreams are often about what we hope for or what we fear or both.

Then just start off with:

> "Once upon a time I was asleep and I had a dream about . . ."

5 ✳ A Story About a Picture

Open a magazine or newspaper to an interesting and, if possible, somewhat ambiguous picture. The whole family can use the same picture or each person can find his or her own. Then each person makes up a story about what could have happened just before this picture was taken. And what will happen next?

6 ✳ If There Were No Parents on Earth

What would you do right now?

7 ✸ WHAT WOULD YOU EAT IF YOU COULD EAT
ANYTHING?

If everything, including toys, furniture and so on,
were safe to eat, what would you nibble on now? What
would it taste like?

Chapter Twenty: Body Language

The creativity sessions in this area ask family members to act out various feelings and create a story for each of them. If a younger child doesn't understand a given feeling, illustrate it for him or her with an experience from that child's past ("You might have felt 'sympathetic,' or sorry for somebody, when your teddy bear fell downstairs," for example).

The purpose is to encourage expressiveness in actions and words, to demonstrate that feelings are valuable and worth recognizing, to teach a few words for common feelings and to have a few family laughs. Younger children may end up imitating older children and parents, but they will at least be getting used to the idea of expressing feelings. (You might begin to point out a variety of facial expressions to them in magazine pictures and on television from now on, too.)

Remember that one or two examples from the lists below are enough for one five-minute Family Creativity Time. And, again, anything goes!

1 ✳ HOW AM I FEELING?

Use your face to express each of the feelings listed below. Then walk and sit as though you were feeling that way. Take turns, beginning with feelings (or "feeling-states") like these:

anger	conceit or being
hurt	"stuck up"
discouragement	excitement
friendliness	worry
irritation	shyness
sympathy	delight
happiness	tiredness
sadness	eagerness
embarrassment	anything else

2 ✳ I Did This Because I Felt That Way

Act out movements and gestures like those below. In each case, make up a story about why you might feel that way. Begin with some like these:

a shrug (e.g., "I didn't care if I got the plastic or the wooden blocks to play with next")	ambling
	shuffling along
	sprawling
	preening
	giving someone the brush-off
a sneer	slumping
a strut	lounging around
a wince	acting shy
a grimace	
hobbling	

Chapter Twenty-One: Say a Poem

These creativity sessions involve several approaches to inventing a poem. They work best if done in consecutive Family Creativity Time sessions, one by one, in approximately the following order—hearing poems, making up "buzz" words, remembering images, creating same-sound sentences, rhythm games, creating metaphors and thinking about special subjects.

The purpose of this series of sessions is to show your family some of the different ways to create poetry, perhaps the most playful use of words. The sessions should help exercise language ability and open everyone's mind to new perceptions.

Have each family member perform each "word play" individually, while others listen. Although some of these resemble some of the Mini-School games, please do not consider them as lessons. Nothing that anybody says is right or wrong.

1 ✳ Listen to Different Kinds of Poems

To jostle any preconceptions about poetry, read to your family, for one Family Creativity Time session, short poems by a wide variety of poets. It doesn't really matter if children understand the poems, just as long as they hear the many different ways in which words can be put together.

Some of the following might make an interesting array of poets—e.e. cummings, Robert Frost, Gerard Manley Hopkins, W. H. Auden, Randall Jarrell, Dylan Thomas, Walt Whitman, William Blake, Wallace Stevens and William Carlos Williams. Their work can be found in any large anthology of poetry.

2 ✳ BUZZ WORDS, OR ONOMATOPOEIA

Tell everyone that poems can sometimes use words that sound like what they are. The word "buzz" sounds like a buzz, for example. Then take turns thinking of others (like sizzle, pop, clop, burp, squeak, ping, boom and so on).

3 ✳ REMEMBER SOMETHING

Tell your family that we can use our memories in poems, too. Take turns thinking of two scenes or images that you remember and especially like. (It could be a shiny garbage can in the sun one spring morning and a smile from your dad before bedtime last week.) Then, share them with each other.

4 ✳ SAME SOUND SENTENCES

Take turns thinking of wild and outrageous phrases or sentences that use mostly the same sound. An example using "S" might be "The silly sun sits on the sofa." Try this with one or two different sounds each time you use this game for Family Creativity Time.

5 ✳ RHYMES

Although many poems have no rhymes at all, the ones your children will see most often in your books do. So have everybody make up rhymes such as, "the goofy is woofy," "the goo-goo boy turned into a blue toy."

6 ✳ SIMILES AND METAPHORS

Take turns thinking of metaphors—how one thing is like another—which is another way to build a poem. Remind everyone to be wild, and begin with comparisons like the following:

> the clouds today are like —— (e.g., scoops of
>   vanilla ice cream, or spilt milk)
> the grass outside is like ——
> that tree's bark is like ——
> the snow is like ——
> these cracks in the sidewalk are like ——
> those bushes are like ——
> that clock's face is like ——
> a crying baby looks like ——
> eating ice cream is like ——
> a dirty house is like ——
> our own carpet is like ——
> buttermilk is like ——
> our linoleum is like ——
> coughing is like ——
> this vegetable tastes as terrible as ——

. . . or any other common object or experience.

7 ✻ SPECIAL SUBJECTS

Remind everyone that a poem can be about anything—dirty dinner dishes, snow forts, love in the
morning, etc. Then, each family member thinks of a very
favorite thing to be the subject of a poem and tells the
others what it will be.

Mention some of the following only if somebody gets
stuck:

my favorite color	flying like a bird
my grandma or grandpa	being a truck
my favorite animal	when I'm happy
the wind today	on my birthday
my blanket	anything

8 ✻ SAY IT

Everyone should think about a special subject and
about how we could use words with interesting sounds to
describe it. Then each person makes up a poem about
that special subject. The poems can be very short and (I
repeat!) don't have to rhyme. Take turns saying them to
each other and, possibly, jotting them down.

Chapter Twenty-Two: Weird Ones

The creativity sessions here provide for your family a potpourri of the almost reasonable to the truly bizarre. They include thinking of alternate uses for common objects, strange outdoor phenomena, new body parts, unusual recipes, nicknames for parents and imaginary countries.

Their purpose is to flex mental muscles, develop a playful mind, even let out a few hostilities and generally have fun together. Let yourself go, taking turns chiming in with as many examples as you can.

Select five minutes worth of activities for each Family Creativity Time session, probably one or two examples from the lists below.

1 ✹ What Else Could You Use It For?

A fireplace could be a raccoon home, a place to grow plants, a wastebasket, a hideout, a sleeping place, a rainwater catcher, a stove, a tree holder, a giant's stand-up resting place, a TV corner and so on.

Now, what else could we do with:

a book?   a shoe?
a chair?   a windowpane?

Mom's car?
your bed?
a card table?
a piece of bread?
a scarf?
the TV set?
apple sauce?
a big box?

cottage cheese?
a huge leaf?
your coat?
a stick?
a blanket?
a hole in the ground?
anything?

2 ✳ AN ALL-NEW OUTDOORS

What could it rain instead of water? How about popcorn, soda pop, marshmallows, leaves, mice, acorns or caramels? Now try the following:

what color should grass be?
what could grow on bushes besides leaves?
what could grow taller than trees?
what could we wear outside in winter instead
    of hats and coats?
what new animals could we have outside and
    what could they do?
what color could the sun be?
what could clouds be made of and how could
    they keep moving?
what new kinds of bugs could we have?
what could lakes, rivers and oceans be filled
    with instead of water?
how could cars look different?
what could streets be made of?
anything?

3 ✳ INVENT A BODY PART

What new part could we have on our bodies and what

would we use it for? (How about a third arm? A TV receiver to bring in pictures? What else?)

4 ✻ RAUCOUS RECIPES

Take turns contributing real ingredients for a wild new recipe with one family member writing them down. Ask each person whether there should be a teaspoon, a tablespoon, or a cup of that ingredient.

Now look it over. Could you conceivably mix it up and/or cook it, perhaps even taste it? If you can, do so. Then taste it—and probably put it out for the squirrels to finish.

5 ✻ NAME THAT PARENT

A good way to express a little friendly hostility is to make up family nicknames. It can also be hilarious. Take turns thinking up ridiculous ones for Dad. Waffle-head? Set him on the table and he'd make a good dinner? Doughnut-nose? Whatever. Then start in on Mom!

6 ✻ WEIRDO COUNTRY

If we each could create a whole new country, what would life be like there? (Mine might rain sunflower seeds, have parents who are smaller than their children, have dogs that eat trash and boast purple trees.) What would be its name?

Chapter Twenty-Three: Make Up a Song

The creativity sessions here encourage your family to break out in song. Depending on their ages, it could be a one-phrase song or a full-blown "post-modern" Christmas carol. The songs can be written by each family member individually—or together, with each person supplying a phrase. They involve creating new tunes for old songs, complete new songs and a family song tree.

Letting loose like a bird can be good for the creative spirit. You may even uncover talents never developed.

Choose five minutes of activities for each Family Creativity Time session.

1   ✻   NEW TUNES FOR OLD SONGS

To shake loose your musical muse, begin by creating a completely new tune for one of the following songs:

"Happy Birthday"
"Twinkle, Twinkle, Little Star"
"America, the Beautiful"
"Glow, Little Glow Worm"
"One Little, Two Little, Three Little Indians"

234

"Puff, the Magic Dragon"
"It's Not That Easy Being Green"
"It's Such a Good Feeling to Know You're
    Alive"

(and whatever your children know from TV, records,
preschool or camp).

2 ✳ WHOLE NEW SONGS

Have each family member choose a subject to write a
song about. It might be "Dinosaurs in Our Yard,"
"Grandma and Grandpa," "Why I Like Christmas," "Ice
Cream and Toy Trucks," "Elephants and Bathtubs,"
"I'm So Mad I Could," etc.

Then each person invents a little song on this subject,
including tune and lyrics. Tape-record them if possible. If
not, jot down the words (and some indication of the tune
if you can) of each song on a small piece of paper.

3 ✳ A FAMILY SONG TREE

Assemble the results from the previous session, preferably after you've done this activity in several different
Family Creativity Time sessions. Then, find an old tree
branch and "plant" it in a flowerpot. Attach to its twigs,
with colored ribbon, the tape cartridges and/or the pieces
of paper displaying the family's songs.

This tree will remind you to play or sing the songs
again. Or it could be a wonderful present for a grand-
parent. It could even become a family memento, especially if you ask the grandparents and great-grandparents to contribute little songs about the children.

In another variant, you could ask the grandparents to

jot down the old traditional nursery songs they sang to *their* children when they were young. And you could add your family favorites, making the tree into a family musical history.

Chapter Twenty-Four: Produce a Show

The creative activities here involve producing, instantly, a puppet show, TV ad, outrageous fairy tale, moving cartoon and radio news report for the family audience. Each is a spontaneous "act it out" activity with essentially no rehearsal.

Their purpose is to introduce your child or children to more of the creative media, the idea of performing (please applaud for each other, even if you all take part) and the fun of sheer creation. Let younger family members perform in each medium first, individually or together, and/or let them tell you what to do. The parents perform afterwards. (I've left "TV *show*" off the list here, although TV ads are included, on the theory that you'd just get a rerun of a program your family has already seen. But add it if you like.)

Choose one of the following types of shows for your five-minute session. And remember—anything goes!

1 ✻ A PUPPET SHOW

Assemble or prepare beforehand some colored socks, abstract paper shapes pasted to old popsicle sticks, store-bought puppets or a combination of all three. To create the stage, tip a table on its side or use a large box. Ask your child or children to use the puppets to tell a story about anything—a weird vacation trip, the day an elephant came to visit, a bad fight, etc. Then give the parents a turn.

2 ✳ A Costumed Play

Assemble the makings of some simple costumes—a fancy dress, a towel, an old necktie, a bathing cap, anything. Let your child or children choose from among these props. Then, alone or together, ask them to put on a play about absolutely anything. (It could be "My First Day At School," "When We Go Swimming," "The Day a Whale Came to Visit" and so on.) After that, the parents perform. (Remember that planning interactions among multiple characters is very hard, even for older preschoolers.)

3 ✳ A TV Ad

Each family member should think of an imaginary product to advertise. It could be purple and green ice cream, polka-dot toothpaste, spinach-flavored shampoo, etc. Then let each person stand up and do a short commercial.

4 ✳ A Goofy Fairy Tale

Each family member should think of a fond fairy tale or nursery rhyme such as the Cinderella story or the "This Little Piggy" limerick. Then take turns standing up and making it wild. For example:

"Prince Lester invited Maggie Flat-

Face to his birthday party, where she left
her diaper and plastic pants and then ran
off. He had to look everywhere to find
her, by matching the pants she left to the
others in her diaper drawer. When he
found her, they celebrated by having beet
soup and bran and opened up some of the
presents. These were a box of wasps, a
bag of banana peels and clean diapers.
Then they played happily ever after."

5 ✳ A Living Cartoon

Cut out a large "cartoon balloon" that looks something like this:

Then, invent one or more new cartoon heroes such as
"Spidergirl," "Dad the Dinosaur," "Gorilla Mom," etc.
Each of your family members then gets a turn to stand
up, hold the cartoon balloon and make up his or her part
of the family cartoon. (Yours might be, "Wow, Spidergirl
whopped Benjy Bunny and ran for the lake.") Keep
going, in turns, until you run out of action for that
cartoon strip. Act it all out if you dare!

6 ✸ A FAMILY RADIO NEWS REPORT

Find something that looks like a microphone and take turns standing up to give your part of the family radio news report on what you did today. Include events you experienced alone as well as those with other family members. Try to use a "radio voice," short sentences and clear facts. Tape it, if you like.

Chapter Twenty-Five: Goofy Words

The creativity sessions in this area encourage your whole family to devise unusual words for familiar objects. (They are, in one sense, an extension of Chapter Seventeen: Name It.) Included are sessions on new names for common items, combination words, unusual names for people, new names for groups of objects and even some "pig latin."

Their purpose is to look at familiar things in new ways, a key ingredient of creativity and a way of making everyday life more interesting. Anything goes, as family members all chime in.

Choose five minutes worth of activities, probably one or two of the examples from the sessions below.

1   ✳   NEW NAMES

Take turns creating new names for common objects—ones that clearly describe what they look like; how they sound, taste or smell; or what we do with them. (If someone comes up with an Indian word you recognize, point that out, too.) Try it with some of these:

moving vans   bananas
cookies   bumblebees

sparrows ("brown
    chirps," "cheep
    birds," "flying
    chocolate chips,"
    etc.)
butterflies
cars
freeways
centipedes, ants or
    cockroaches
sofas

sidewalks
peaches
milk
crackers
lakes
cottage cheese
the laundry room
wheat germ
skyscrapers
whatever

2 ✻ COMBO WORDS

Think of *single* words to describe the longer phrases commonly used in your family. ("Time to go to the bathroom," for example, might become, "Timebath" or "Goroom.") Write them down—some might catch on within your family. After all, a language identifies a culture, and a family is surely a mini-culture.

3 ✻ SILLY NAMES

Take turns making up outlandish names for imaginary people. Get started with "Annie Armpit," "Schnickelfritz Steptoe," "Carrot-Nose Carrothers," and so on.

4 ✻ GROUP NAMES

Take turns creating new ways of identifying groups of objects. Instead of "a flight of stairs" (which was once probably quite unusual and creative), say "a bump thump of stairs," for example. Try it with some of the following:

—— of books
—— of children
—— of cars
—— of adults
—— of teachers
—— of monkeys
—— of grackles
—— of brothers and
    sisters
—— of seals

—— of trucks
—— of felt-tipped
    pens
—— of elephants
—— of records
—— of dogs
—— of airplanes
—— of ducks
—— of TV sets

. . . and so on.

5 ✳ PIG LATIN

This language game from everybody's youth is fun for sound play if your child or children are old enough. The word "play" becomes "lay-pay," for example, and "home" becomes "ome-hay" as you take off the first letter of each word, add an "ay" to it and place it after the remaining portion of the original word. Talk it up a little!

Chapter Twenty-Six: Make a Family Book

This creativity project, which requires several sequential Family Creativity Time sessions, culminates in a family book. It should be worth doing—and saving!

It requires creative thinking and family cooperation, along with enough discipline to finish a project. It need not be long, but it should be completed eventually.

Spend as many five-minute sessions as you need to (probably five or six), with each family member primarily responsible for completing each task.

1 ✹ CHOOSE A SUBJECT AND TITLE

Brainstorm for a subject and a title. The book could be about virtually anything that your family could conceivably experience together. It might be a birthday party, an invasion of a wild animal, a bizarre adventure trip or the day you ruled the world. Using these suggestions the title could be "Wild Birthdays Are Forever," "The Day the Skunk Climbed Down the Chimney," "Our Rocket Trip to Venus" or "When the Smiths Were King." Come to a decision together.

2 ✹ MAKE THE COVER

With as much help from your child or children as

possible, write the title, list the family members as co-authors, name an imaginary publishing company and create the art for the cover.

3 ✳ CREATE THE STORY

Following the "family pot-boiler" method, take turns adding phrases or sentences to the story—the more outrageous the better. A parent should jot it all down quickly so that, later, family members can write it carefully, one sentence to a page. (Slowing down the pace at this point would spoil the spontaneity of the story creation.)

4 ✳ WRITE IT DOWN

Take turns writing down the story, about one sentence per page.

5 ✳ ILLUSTRATE AND DECORATE IT

Each family member should illustrate and decorate his or her share of the pages, using virtually any media or methods. (How about finger paint, collage, felt-tipped pen, real marigold or other flowers, fruit smear, water colors, crayons, a dab of perfume, charcoal or colored pencils?)

Then staple it all together and applaud each other. It's your book!

Afterword

As you and your child use this book, you may gradually come to think of yourself as a teacher. Like a teacher, you might want to record your child's progress—jotting down or checking off the learning games mastered, the ones in need of review, etc. Also, please don't forget to reward your child for especially good sessions in Mini-School and Family Creativity Time—not with grades, of course, but with extra hugs, small special privileges or treats, even with cardboard star badges or stickers.

Reward yourself somehow, too. After all, you are your child's best and favorite teacher.